Personal Well-Being
Lessons for Secondary
Schools

Praise for this book

"Boniwell and Ryan provide an excellent synopsis of the current state of wellbeing literature focusing on evidence-based studies and how these link into contemporary public policy. This underpins the work that Boniwell and Ryan have done to ensure that the 'hands-on' methodology outlined throughout the text is underscored by science that highlights the importance of each exercise. Students are encouraged by this design to take a long term view of their development.

Boniwell and Ryan's text is a significant contribution to the growing area of Wellbeing and Positive Education literature. Its teacher friendly format and engaging exercises will stimulate many classroom discussions."

Dr Mathew A White, Director, Wellbeing & Positive Education, St Peter's College, Australia and Fellow, Melbourne Graduate School of Education, University of Melbourne, Australia

"This book is a much welcomed addition to the field of student well-being. The authors have captured the science and practice of positive psychology and have brought together an array of evidence-based practices and exercises that will allow teachers to explicitly incorporate well-being into their curriculum and pastoral care. The 6 areas of well-being are scientifically validated and the book provides excellent resources and teaching tips. The comprehensive list of classroom activities will positively impact upon the well-being of secondary students. This book is an asset to any teacher who believes in 'whole-student' learning."

Lea Waters, Associate Professor, University of Melbourne, Australia

"This book does exactly as promised by the title. Providing practical, exciting, creative, and stimulating lesson plans for students, on the subject of well-being and, indeed, life skills, informed by the best available evidence from Positive Psychology. The lessons are comprehensive, excellently presented for teachers, all supported by clear explanations of the research evidence and concepts, and have the benefit of active student engagement and participation. This book provides a flexible and accessible source book of wonderful ideas and activities. Given the importance of student well-being, and their emotional, social and personal development, as well as their basic happiness, this book would be valuable for every Secondary School and Academy."

Professor Irvine S. Gersch, University of East London, UK

"Ilona Boniwell and Lucy Ryan's book is exactly what teachers require. 'It fits with the teachers' needs in terms of how and what to teach when positive education is a concern. The different aspects of their program are detailed in 36 lessons, with theoretical background and practical tips, the 'Lesson Plan' and 'How to' parts, which are very useful. This structure is very convenient. This is not only a book but also a very interesting tool designed for each teacher in charge of pupils aged from 11 to 14."

Dr Charles Martin-Krumm, University Western Brittany, France

"A very useful compendium of PSHE-type activities."

Guy Claxton, University of Winchester, UK

Personal Well-Being Lessons for Secondary Schools

Positive psychology in action
for 11 to 14 year olds

Ilona Boniwell and Lucy Ryan

Open University Press

Open University Press
McGraw-Hill Education
McGraw-Hill House
Shoppenhangers Road
Maidenhead
Berkshire
England
SL6 2QL

email: enquiries@openup.co.uk
world wide web: www.openup.co.uk

and

Two Penn Plaza, New York, NY 10121-2289, USA

Open University Press 2012

A catalogue record of this book is available from the British Library

ISBN10: 0335246168 (pb)
ISBN13: 9780335246168 (pb)
eISBN: 9780335246175

Library of Congress Cataloging-in-Publication Data
CIP data has been applied for

Typeset by Aptara Inc., India

Printed and bound by CPI Group (UK) Ltd, Croydon, CR0 4YY

The **McGraw·Hill** Companies

Contents

Introduction

The true measure of a nation's standing is how well it attends to its children – their health and safety, their material security, their education and socialization, and their sense of being loved, valued, and included in the families into which they are born.

(UNICEF 2007)

What is well-being education and why should we have it?

It is likely that the first decade of the twenty-first century will be viewed by historians as a landmark decade for the explicit development of children's well-being. Once implicit in the education of children, well-being has now become an overt government agenda in many countries across the world. For instance, the primary objective of the UK Government's 'Every Child Matters' initiative, underpinned by the Children's Act (2004), is to 'Safeguard children and young people, improve their life outcomes and general well-being' (DfES 2007b, p. 35). More recently, the UK Department for Children, Schools and Families published *The Children's Plan*, setting ten new targets to improve children's well-being by 2020, through nurturing 'happy, capable and resilient children' (DCSF 2007, p. 5).

The reasons for the focus on the development of well-being in children are twofold. We are forced to recognize that Western countries are currently facing an unprecedented increase in childhood and adolescent depression. At any point in time, approximately 2 per cent of children aged 11–15 and 11 per cent of youth aged 16–24 in the UK are suffering a major depressive disorder (Green et al. 2005). Anxiety disorders, which often precede and co-occur with depression, are found in approximately 3 per cent of children aged 5–15 and 15 per cent of youth aged 16–24 (Green et al. 2005). In the USA, approximately one in five adolescents has a major depressive episode by the end of high school (Lewinsohn et al., 1993), with a similar picture observed in Australia (Noble and McGrath 2005). Children and adolescents who suffer from high levels of depressive symptoms or depressive disorders are more likely to have academic and interpersonal difficulties. They are more likely to smoke, use drugs and alcohol, and attempt suicide (Garrison et al. 1991; Covey et al. 1998). The wealth of the countries appears to provide relatively little protection for their youth. Recent international attempts to directly measure child well-being offer a worrying picture. The 2007 UNICEF report, which presents an overview of child well-being in rich countries, sees the UK occupying the bottom third in the list of 21 industrialized countries (UNICEF 2007). Of primary importance to this report is Dimension 6 – Subjective Well Being – in which children ranked their opinion of their health, their liking for school and their subjective view of their personal well-being. The United Kingdom came last in this dimension, causing a rich debate on the success of current welfare and education policies. Bob Reitemeier, the Chief Executive of The Children's Society, reported in *The Guardian* on February 14, 2007: 'Unicef's report is a wake-up call to the fact that, despite being a rich country, the UK is failing children and young people in a number of crucial ways.'

Although the case for well-being education can be made purely on the basis of prevention of ill-health, depression, anxiety and other mental health disorders, there is at least as much value in appreciating the benefits that well-being can bring. Already in 1947 the World Health Organization (WHO) defined health in terms of wellness, that is: physical, mental, and social well-being, not merely the absence of disease (WHO 1947). A substantial body of research documents the advantages of well-being and positive individual characteristics. For instance, research demonstrates that happy people are successful across multiple life domains, including marriage, relationships, health, longevity, income and work performance. They are more creative, able to multi-task and endure boring tasks, are more trusting, helpful and sociable (Lyubomirsky et al. 2005). Those able to identify, develop and use their strengths, and are more likely to be high achievers (Buckingham and Coffman, 1999), while higher levels of grit or self-discipline in children predict academic success over and above their IQ levels (Duckworth and Seligman 2005).

Well-being education aims to develop the skills of well-being, flourishing and optimal functioning in children, teenagers and students. In so doing, it focuses on both the preventative and enabling or developmental functions. Importantly, well-being education is underpinned by principles and methods of empirical validation, which is what differentiates psychological science from self-help initiatives.

Well-being education from a historical perspective

Since the late 1800s, educators have been divided about education's purpose and its potential for the academic, moral, emotional and social development of learners. For much of the twentieth century, Western countries have focused on traditional conceptions of knowledge based on academic subject groups, e.g. maths, geography and music. Increasingly educators felt the emotional aspects of learning were neglected, prompting school leaders to reconsider the curricular needs of young people. Programmes were developed to meet particular needs arising as new social issues arose or 'soft skills' were needed. Schools in the USA, the UK, Australia and across the world have for some time included work on social and emotional issues in the curriculum (e.g. Personal, Social and Health Education, Service Learning, Citizenship) and helped pupils reflect on the importance of good social and emotional skills. This section provides a brief overview of the prominent frameworks for positive education that have been implemented over the past half a century, positioning this book in multi-faceted approaches to well-being education as broadly defined.

This section will also mention a number of discrete programmes currently prominent in English-speaking countries, including the UK, the USA and Australia (although some of these have been translated into other languages and introduced in other countries).

The self-esteem movement

The social and emotional lives of school-aged young people became a focus in education in the 1970s with the emergence of the self-esteem movement. This movement was derived from the core principles of humanistic psychology, and began to impact on teachers' practices in the classroom and parents' child-rearing practices. Classroom self-esteem programmes typically focused on the importance of helping children gain a sense of achievement in a relatively non-competitive and failure-free learning environment, and to engage in self-expression. Children were encouraged by both teachers and parents to see themselves as special and unique. 'Low self-esteem' was widely regarded as an explanation for many social 'ills' such as juvenile crime, teenage pregnancy, substance abuse and low academic achievement. Yet Twenge (2007) documents increases in anxiety among young people since the 1970s that she associates with systematic techniques used in schools to 'boost' self-esteem.

Nowadays, concerns about the self-esteem movement's focus on 'feeling good' and individualism are also shared by Martin Seligman, the founder of positive psychology. He claims that the movement has probably contributed to the increase in depression in young people:

> Armies of . . . teachers, along with . . . parents, are straining to bolster children's self-esteem. That sounds innocuous enough, but the way they do it often erodes children's sense of worth. By emphasizing how a child feels, at the expense of what the child does – mastery, persistence, overcoming frustration and boredom and meeting a challenge – parents and teachers are making this generation of children more vulnerable to depression.
>
> *(Seligman et al. 1995, p. 27)*

Seligman argues that if children are not allowed to fail or be disappointed with themselves, and if they receive less-than-genuine praise, then they are deprived of opportunities to develop frustration, tolerance and persistence and are less motivated to work harder.

Various reviews of the self-esteem literature have found little evidence that developing young people's self-esteem makes a significant difference to student academic achievement, their mental health or societal problems (e.g., Kahne 1996; Baumeister et al. 2003; Emler 2003). Baumeister, a former proponent of the self-esteem movement, concluded from the results of his own research and a meta-review of earlier studies that the widespread assumption that artificially enhancing self-esteem would reduce young people's problems and increase their achievement was plainly false. Despite these findings, the self-esteem movement continued for many years and is only now beginning to fade:

> While the self-esteem movement has been largely debunked, we are just now reaping what it has sown. The generation raised under these conditions is entering the workforce and has been described as difficult and that their expectations far exceed those of their predecessors in entry level positions. The praise they have been given all of their lives is still expected, even if they have not done anything to earn it and they lack the resiliency to deal with real disappointment and the realities of life.
>
> *(LaPorta, 2009, p. 5)*

Resilience education

There are many different definitions of resilience but all of them, in one way or another refer to the capacity of the individual to 'overcome odds' and demonstrate the personal strengths needed to cope with some kind of hardship or adversity. Resilience has been described as the ability to persist, cope adaptively and bounce back after encountering change, challenges, setback, disappointments, difficult situations or adversity and to return to a reasonable level of well-being (McGrath and Noble 2003). Benard (2004) suggests resilience is also a set of qualities or protective mechanisms that give rise to successful adaptation by a young person despite high risk factors during the course of their development.

The construct of resilience emerged about 40 years ago, almost by accident, from longitudinal developmental studies of 'at risk' children. This research showed that, despite encountering many major life stressors as they grew up, some children survived and even thrived (Werner and Smith 1992). The well-being and resilience research has shifted the focus from those children who are casualties of these risk factors to those children who manage to bounce back from stress, trauma and risk in their lives. The resilience construct is thus a dramatic change in perspective from a deficit model of young people 'at risk' to a model that focuses on teaching the personal skills and developing the environmental contexts that help young people withstand high levels of 'risk'. Research has now been able to identify the most significant coping skills and protective life circumstances that help young people to become more resilient (e.g., Benard 2004). After families, schools are the most likely place where students can experience the protective environmental conditions and learn the social-emotional skills that enhance resilience. In fact, for young people who do not experience family support, school may be the only place where they can learn those skills. Teaching these skills can also inoculate them against the possibility of not coping when faced with future difficulties or adversity, just as vaccinations can inoculate them against the possibility of being adversely affected by exposure to future disease. A substantial number of school-based programmes emerged following the development of these ideas.

The Penn Resiliency Programme (PRP) is a schools-based intervention curriculum designed to increase resilience and promote optimism, adaptive coping skills and effective problem-solving through the applications of the principles of cognitive behavioural therapy to normal populations. Based on the seven 'learnable' skills of resilience, the programme teaches children: how to identify their feelings; tolerance of ambiguity; the optimistic explanatory style; how to analyse causes of problems; empathy; self-efficacy; and how to reach out or try new things. The PRP, therefore, educates adolescents to challenge a habitual pessimistic explanatory style by looking at the evidence and considering what is realistic, while avoiding unrealistic optimism. The PRP has been developed and researched for over 16 years and consequently has acquired a solid base of evidence (Reivich and Shatté 2002; Seligman 2002, 2007; Reivich et al. 2007). A meta-analysis of 17 controlled evaluations of the programme found participants reported fewer depressive symptoms up to one year after the programme in comparison to young people who had received no intervention (Brunwasser et al. 2009). However, the PRP is essentially preventative in nature with the expressed aim of reducing depression among teenagers. For students whose future functioning is more positive, the programme is beneficial, however, it is difficult to see whether it is beneficial for students not at risk of depression.

A further applied classroom resiliency programme is *Bounce Back!* Devised by two Australian psychologists, Dr Helen McGrath and Dr Toni Noble (McGrath and Noble 2003), it is a highly practical, teacher-friendly programme. It is based on the conclusions, reached by a meta-review of schools-based programmes, that the benefits of the vast majority of short-term programmes are, in fact, not sustainable. Bounce Back! is delivered in both primary and secondary schools, revisiting fundamental concepts in developmentally appropriate ways over time. Emerging research evidence indicates beneficial effects of the programme on depression (McGrath and Noble 2003).

An alternative programme, *Zippy's Friends*, is an international 24-week school curriculum that teaches all students a set of coping skills designed to improve future relationships and mental well-being. Meta-analysis of the programme's evaluation reports at least small positive effects for each implementation of the programme (Durlak and Wells 1997). However, evaluated programmes tend to have small sample sizes and use 'expert' teachers for implementation (Mishara and Ystgaard 2006). Given that research clearly shows that the quality of a teacher impacts on student well-being and achievement regardless of the subject, it is difficult to discern whether positive student outcomes from Zippy's Friends are due to the content of the lessons on coping skills or due to students receiving the attention of a high-quality teacher (Hattie 2003).

Finally, the *SPARK Resilience Programme* is a new addition to the world of preventative positive education. Developed for and piloted in deprived neighbourhoods of East London, the programme builds on research findings from four relevant fields of study: cognitive behavioural therapy, resilience, post-traumatic growth, and positive psychology. Organized around the SPARK acronym, it teaches students to break simple and complex situations into manageable components of a Situation, Perception, Autopilot, Reaction and Knowledge. Through the use of hypothetical scenarios informed by consultations with students in pilot schools, students learn how an everyday *Situation* can trigger in them an *Autopilot* (feelings and emotions). These *Autopilots* vary for different people and different circumstances because of the unique way we *Perceive* these *Situations*. We then *React* to the *Situation* and learn something from it, that is, we acquire *Knowledge* about the way we are, or others are, or the world is. To help students understand these concepts, they are introduced to 'parrots of perception' – imaginary creatures representing common distortions of human cognition and thinking. The programme teaches students how to challenge their interpretation of any life situation and consider other alternatives by putting their parrots 'on trial', understanding their automatic emotional responses and learning to control their non-constructive behavioural reactions. Alongside, they are introduced to the skills of assertiveness and problem-solving, and are helped to build their 'resilience muscles' through identifying their strengths, social support networks, sources of positive emotions and previous experiences of resilience. The statistical data analysis showed significantly higher resilience, self-esteem and self-efficacy scores in the post-assessment compared to the pre-assessment data. A marginally significant decrease was also observed in depression symptoms (Boniwell et al. in preparation).

Although being able to decrease depression and anxiety in children and adolescents is a striking achievement that cannot be understated, the above programmes may be charged with not going far enough in enhancing well-being, rather than simply alleviating possible psychological problems. Well-being is not a mere absence of depression, just as the person who is not ill is not necessarily in good physical shape. Development of well-being needs to include skills over and above successful coping, including the enhancement of positive emotions, flow, positive relations and meaningfulness.

The SEL (Social and Emotional Learning) movement

Over the past 15 years the social and emotional learning (SEL) movement has been slowly replacing the self-esteem movement. Daniel Goleman popularized the notion of emotional intelligence in the 1990s, In his best-selling book (*Emotional Intelligence*, 1996), he drew on Howard Gardner's earlier work on the multiple intelligences model (Gardner 1983, 1999) and Salovey et al.'s (2004) work on emotional intelligence. The social and emotional learning (SEL) model developed by CASEL (Collaboration for Academic and Social-Emotional Learning) at the University of Illinois is based on Goleman's framework. SEL differs from the self-esteem movement in many ways but, most importantly, there is some research evidence to support the claim that schools-based SEL programmes can increase student achievement, build their connection to school, improve their interpersonal attitudes and behaviours, and decrease negative behaviours, such as violence and substance abuse, and that these outcomes occur across a wide range of diverse students and settings and persist over time (Zins et al. 2007). Social and emotional learning programmes have been described as among the most successful interventions ever offered to school-aged young people (Payton et al. 2008).

The following social and emotional skills have also been identified by the Collaboration for Academic, Social, and Emotional Learning (CASEL 2010) as the foci of intervention programmes: self-awareness, self-management, social awareness, relationship skills and responsible decision-making.

The *Primary SEAL* (Social and Emotional Aspects of Learning) programme is a UK social and emotional whole-school initiative for primary students, which involves classroom teachers introducing social and emotional skills in order to enhance student relationships, attendance, behaviour, learning and emotional well-being (DFES 2005). It has been adopted in 80 per cent of British schools (Humphrey et al. 2008). SEAL is a universal approach but also includes early intervention with small learning groups for students who are deemed to need extra support and follow-up individual interventions with those students who do not appear to have benefited from either the whole-class programme or the small groups for early interventions. The themes in the program are New Beginnings (emotional literacy), Going for Goals (self-regulation and empathy), Getting On and Falling Out (social skills), Say No to Bullying, and Good to Be Me. The results of extensive evaluation look to be promising (Humphrey et al. 2008), and the programme is now supplemented by *Secondary SEAL*.

Positive psychology movement

Positive psychology (PP) is the science of positive aspects of human life, such as happiness, well-being and flourishing. Often contrasted with the medical model, this approach places an explicit emphasis on the potential of individuals and on researching things that make life worth living (Seligman and Csikszentmihalyi 2000). PP poses slightly different questions, such as 'What works?' rather than 'What doesn't work?'; asks 'What is right with this person?' rather than 'What is wrong?'; asks 'Why do some individuals succeed when faced with unfavourable circumstances?' instead of 'Why do people some fail?'. In a nutshell, PP can be summarized as drawing on what is strong, rather than dealing with what is wrong.

A stronger focus on well-being in general and on student well-being in particular has evolved from the positive psychology movement. Like the self-esteem movement, positive psychology incorporates some of the principles of humanistic psychology. However, unlike the self-esteem movement, positive psychology is significantly supported by research (Seligman 2007). Positive psychology, as the name implies, focuses on positives, namely those strengths and behaviours that enable people to have robust levels of well-being and enable individuals, groups and organizations to thrive. Positive psychology researchers study the positive effects of a range of factors on well-being/happiness including: positive emotions (Frederickson 2001); engagement and 'psychological flow' (Csikszentmihalyi 2000); the identification and building of personal character strengths (Peterson and Seligman, 2004) and intellectual strengths (Gardner 1999; McGrath and Noble 2003); optimistic thinking (Seligman et al. 1995), and having a sense of meaning and purpose (Seligman 2002).

With the expansion of the positive psychology field, the past decade has seen a surprising wealth of curricula being developed around the world to address different aspects of positive functioning. For example, the *Wisdom Curriculum* encourages the intellectual and moral development of children through the medium of mainstream subjects (Reznitskaya and Sternberg 2004). A number of projects accentuating hope in schoolchildren include *Making Hope Happen* and *Making Hope Happen for Kids* (Lopez et al. 2004). A strengths-based development programme, developed by the Gallup Foundation, has been found to significantly improve academic performance (Hodges and Clifton. 2004). In the UK, the *Celebrating Strengths* approach, targeting the development of strengths through storytelling, has been implemented in primary schools in the north of England (Eades 2008). Emotional intelligence has been widely used as an umbrella concept for various programmes that teach social and emotional learning, the most successful of which are *Self Science* and *The South Africa Emotional Intelligence Curriculum* (Salovey et al. 2004). Some of the programmes, such as *Going for the Goal*, that teaches adolescents the skills of positive goal setting and facilitation of goal attainment, have been carried out on a very large scale (Danish 1996). Key School, in Indianapolis, in the USA, aims to cultivate pupils' experience of flow (full engagement in an activity). Their programme provides opportunities for pupils to challenge their abilities, and the school has a Flow Activities Center, where pupils have the time and space to engage in activities related to their own interests. The Culver Academies, a group of boarding high schools in Indiana, have integrated character strengths and positive emotions throughout the school. Teaching staff have been trained in strengths and positive emotions, and staff performance reviews are based on the strengths approach (Yeager 2007). The Hawn Foundation, a US charity, has developed a mindfulness education curriculum that was being piloted in schools in Canada and the USA in 2008.

In September 2006, Wellington College – a private, co-educational school in the UK – embarked on a two-year *Skills of Well-Being* programme for its pupils. The course was designed by Ian Morris and Dr Nick Baylis and is delivered fortnightly to Years 10 and 11 (ages 14–16) with the specific aim of 'redressing the imbalance in modern education caused by an emphasis on exam results and measured outcomes' (Baylis and Morris 2006, p. 3). The ultimate outcome of the course is to give Wellington College pupils practical skills for living well that are useful, easily understood and can be applied on a daily basis. Although the course is still developing, the passionate desire to deliver these skills is driving an ongoing review of the course. This is coupled with an intention to avoid a 'myopic' approach and broaden the breadth and depth of the course to include knowledge from positive psychology, drawing on the latest evidence-based research and practical interventions. Skills of Well-Being has, at present, very limited scientific validation. Despite this fact, it has attracted unprecedented media coverage, placing the well-being debate firmly at the heart of the British political agenda.

In the USA, a programme of 17 lessons, each two hours in length, was developed to introduce positive psychology to high school students. Developed on ideas in Martin Seligman's (2002) book, *Authentic Happiness*, and including a substantial resilience component, the programme incorporates several tested and innovative positive psychology interventions, such as savouring (Bryant and Veroff 2006), gratitude letters and counting blessings (Seligman et al. 2005), and forgiveness and letting go of grudges (McCullough and Witvliet 2000).

Our book is based on the *Well-Being Curriculum* for primary and secondary schools that has been piloted in the UK for at least three years at the time of printing. The Well-Being Curriculum is a joint project of the partnership between the Haberdashers' Aske's Academies Federation and the University of East London (UEL). The partnership has developed a comprehensive well-being curriculum based on the principles and findings of positive psychology and taught weekly to students from Year 1 to Year 13. The curriculum targets every known major predictor and correlate of well-being, using individually tested interventions to enhance learning. The emphasis of the curriculum in Years 1–9 is on positive interventions, targeting areas that have a substantial evidence base such as happiness, positive emotions, flow, resilience, achievement, positive relationships and meaning. The emphasis in Years 10–13 is on positive education, enabling young people to reflect upon and make choices about their well-being and development. This four-part curriculum spans four years, focusing on the areas of self, being, doing and relationships. Pilot evaluation of the programme showed increases in various aspects of well-being (i.e. positive affect, satisfaction with friends, and satisfaction with oneself) consistent with the areas targeted (Boniwell and Osin, in preparation).

Effective planning for well-being education

Although it is difficult to define what makes a good school, researchers agree that it is a type of school that encourages students to be engaged with and enthusiastic about learning. Common features of such schools include a safe environment, an articulated and shared vision of the school's purpose, explicit goals for students, emphasis on the individual student, and rewarding their efforts or improvements (Peterson 2006). Student satisfaction with the school, feelings of security and belonging play a crucial role in their engagement in learning and achievement (Brand et al. 2003). Furthermore, the available research evidence strongly indicates the following seven principles for the effective implementation of well-being lessons in schools (Noble and McGrath, in press).

1 Programmes that are taught by class teachers are more likely to be effective

Academic, social and emotional improvements are more likely to occur when teachers (rather than external consultants or professionals) implement a relevant programme (Weissberg and O'Brien 2004; CASEL 2010).

2 The programme should be acceptable to teachers

A schools-based programme that is actually liked by the teachers who teach it is more likely to be effective (Elliott et al. 1991; Eckert and Hinze, 2000; McDougal et al. 2000). Teacher acceptance reflects their perception that the programme seems to be worth their time and effort, feasible, socially valid (Gresham and Lopez 1996) and consistent with their educational, psychological and social perspectives and classroom practices. It also reflects their perception that they have the necessary competencies to teach the programme (Nastasi 2002). This is the reason why both the PRP and SPARK Resilience Programmes focus on teaching adult resilience skills to teachers first to ensure their buy-in.

3 Universal programmes are more effective

A universal programme is delivered to all students, not just those who are identified as 'at risk' for mental health problems. A universal programme reflects the paradigm shift in education, social welfare and psychology from just targeting students at risk to giving some protective skills to all students (Greenberg et al. 2001; Benard 2004; CASEL 2010). Universal programmes can also incorporate options for additional targeted learning with indicated students. This book is a good example of such a programme.

4 Programmes that are long-term and even multi-year have more chance of success

Short-term preventive interventions produce time-limited benefits. Whole-year or multi-year programmes are more likely to produce enduring benefits and are more sustainable especially when taught across age levels (Greenberg et al. 2001; Greenberg et al. 2003; Wells et al. 2003). The programme offered by this book is one-year long, but can potentially be split into two years.

5 A multi-strategic approach is more effective than a single highly focused approach

A multi-strategic approach involves the inclusion of a collection of coordinated 'active ingredients' rather than a single focus (Kellerman et al. 1998; Greenberg et al. 2001; Catalano et al., 2003). The proposed programme contains six major subject streams, all underlined by research evidence regarding their respective contribution to well-being.

6 Effective programmes include a significant component of skills derived from cognitive behavioural approaches (CBT)

There is substantial research support for the efficacy of cognitive behavioural therapy (CBT) in constructively changing feelings and behaviour (e.g., Andrews et al. 2001; Andrews et al. 2002;

Scheckner et al. 2002). CBT, which was originally developed by Aaron Beck (Beck et al. 1979), is based on the understanding that how you think affects how you feel which in turn influences how you behave. The premise is that by adopting more positive and rational thinking, you can help yourself to change your behaviour. A number of lessons in this book (e.g. Lesson 20, Hope, and Lesson 24, Think Yourself Happier) involve some elements of CBT.

7 The programme should incorporate evidence-based teaching strategies

If a programme is to be successfully embedded in the curriculum, then it must include not only evidence-based psychological approaches but must also incorporate evidence-based teaching strategies. Cooperative learning techniques, suggested throughout this book, have extensive evidence support for improving academic outcomes as well as building positive relationships, class cohesion and social-emotional learning (e.g. Marzano et al. 2001; Roseth et al. 2008; Hattie 2009). The use of high-quality literature as an entry point for discussions on well-being topics can also serve to meet literacy outcomes. Other teaching strategies such as educational games, where students work in pairs or small groups against other pairs in the class (e.g., Hattie 2009), and participation in class discussion (Lowen 2003) also actively engage students in learning, develop positive relationships and teach social-emotional skills.

Organization of this book

The aim of the book is to provide educators with a grounded and flexible resource for teaching 11–15-year-olds through a series of up to 36 well-being lessons. Each lesson contains:

● a suggested 60-minute outline Lesson Plan;

● How To instructions on running the lesson;

● handouts for students that can be downloaded from the website, www.openup.co.uk/positivepsychology;

● PowerPoint slides when suggested by the lesson (located on the dedicated website);

● references and resources.

The website address is www.openup.co.uk/positivepsychology and in the text, a mouse icon will indicate that the relevant handout is to be found on the website.

Following the basic premise of the book, all lessons are grounded in scientific discoveries related to well-being. Therefore, notes running alongside the How To part of the lessons are designed to inform teachers of the psychological theory and empirical findings behind suggested activities and interventions.

We believe that the need for flexibility when running such a curriculum is paramount. Educators have many demands on their time and while running a full 36-hour positive psychology programme may be desirable, a 'dip-in' resource for a smaller scale programme gives it a unique edge. Therefore, the book is divided into six subject headings (as per the model delineated below) with six lessons offered per each subject stream. This means the reader can run a programme consisting of 6, 12, 18, 24 or 36 lessons, taking either 1, 2, 3, 4 or 6 lessons from each subject heading. Alternatively, one may choose to run one or two streams in their entirety.

The six subject streams are as follows (see the Positive Psychology in Action Lessons Grid):

1. Positive Self

2. Positive Body

3. Positive Emotions

4. Positive Mindset

5. Positive Direction

6. Positive Relationships

Positive Self

This stream combines lessons related to the nature of happiness and well-being (Happy Talk (Lesson 1)) with lessons on confidence and self-efficacy (Me, Inc. (Lesson 2) and Confident You (Lesson 4)). My Best Possible Self (Lesson 5) is centred on an exercise that is known to enhance well-being in the long term, while the My Strengths Portfolio (Lesson 3) and The Strengths Songbook (Lesson 6) play out the idea of strengths – our positive traits, the exercise of which is also known to contribute to the life well lived.

Positive Body

Not surprisingly, our physical state plays a major part in the way we feel psychologically. In fact, recent advances in research demonstrate that exercise, for example (The Power of Exercise (Lesson 12)) is a much better antidote for depression than any anti-depressant medication. Our diet is, without doubt, another important contributor (see Supersize Me! (Lesson 8) and The Nutrition Quiz (Lesson 9)). However, the flipside to healthy eating is dieting for the sake of body image, which can sometimes be taken to extreme (hence Image Matters (Lesson 7)). This stream also addresses healthy sleep and some strategies for getting it (Go to Bed, Sleepyhead! (Lesson 11)), as well as the basics of mindfulness and meditation – ancient techniques of balance that have a surprising recent history of scientific discoveries associated with them (Mindfulness for Life (Lesson 10)).

Positive Emotions

Emotions are inseparable from the very notion of happiness, since well-being is often defined as the presence of positive and the absence of negative emotions. This stream focuses on the important adaptive functions of both positive and negative emotions (Understanding Emotions (Lesson 13)), the main enemy of positivity – the Negativity Bias (Lesson 14) – our tendency to easily notice negative events, things and people, and ways of dealing with it. Other lessons teach students the value of positive emotions (Boost your Positive Emotions! (Lesson 15)) and humour (Just for Fun (Lesson 17)), as well as ways to enhance them through savouring (Surprising, Spontaneous Savouring!) and positive reminiscence (Mental Time Travelling (Lesson 18)).

Positive Mindset

The psychology of well-being is not short of techniques helping us to train our minds to actually see the world as a glass that is half-full, such as Hope (Lesson 20), Creative Problem-Solving (Lesson 21) or other activities we consciously embark upon (Think Yourself Happier (Lesson 24)). But first of all, it is important to challenge our fixed ways of thinking (Fixed or Flexible? (Lesson 19)), our preconceptions about the importance of money (Money, Money, Money (Lesson 22)) and even choice (The Tyranny of Choice (Lesson 23)).

Positive Direction

This stream is all about motivation (Egg Yourself On (Lesson 25)), self-regulation or will power (Nail, Nag, Nudge (Lesson 26)) and goal setting (Big Hairy Goals (Lesson 28)) on the way to achieve optimal engagement (The Flow Zone (Lesson 27)). An essential element of being able to direct oneself is time management (Five Little Pigs (Lesson 29)) and achieving balance between freely chosen and necessary activities (The Balancing Act (Lesson 30)).

Positive Relationships

It is well known that relationships are at the very core of our well-being, regardless of whether we are introverts or extraverts. This stream focuses on the basic relationships skills, such as being able to form and maintain friendships (Tonic or Toxic? (Lesson 31)), being able to listen and, even more importantly, to hear (Listening and Empathy (Lesson 33)) and negotiation skills (Sweet Trading (Lesson 34)). Forgiveness (Lesson 32), Kindness and Gratitude (Lesson 35) are also included, as the main relationship strengths. The stream finishes with Happiness across Cultures (Lesson 36) – a lesson that highlights factors that allow countries to flourish, taking the scope of relationships to the planetary level.

Working on the ground: delivering well-being lessons

Lessons in this book are designed to be delivered in the spirit of participation, open-mindedness and inquiry. Most of activities are fun and engaging, and have already been tried and enjoyed by students of relevant age.

However, there are certain behaviours that can be disruptive and not facilitative to the classroom atmosphere. We feel that it may be helpful to make some suggestions how such behaviours can be confronted in a constructive way. Of course, these are not 'rules', and teachers are encouraged to use their own experience in dealing with such situations.

Disruptive behaviour (being late, chatting to others, using mobile phone, etc.)

Before beginning these series of lessons, it might help to agree on the ground rules with the whole class, occasionally reminding participants about these ground rules when disruptive behaviour occurs. When a student is late, the teacher should first finish something that has already been started before acknowledging the newcomer, inquiring about the reasons for being late and summarizing in a brief form what has been done so far. If students are chatting, one may invite them to share their comments with the whole class. If disruptions continue, it might be worth having a talk with the participant(s) after the session to inquire about the reasons for disruptions. Some possible consequences of such behaviour may need to be outlined at this point. These, ultimately, may involve a student's removal from the class (better to lose one person than the whole class).

Expressing hostility, criticizing everything, questioning to 'catch' the presenter

In this situation, the first rule is to keep calm. However, this does not mean tolerating abusive behaviour (otherwise it will grow). The student may be confronted calmly and asked why they behave in such a way. Another solution is to acknowledge the point and agree to differ, without engaging in an argument about it, or offer to discuss the issue after the lesson. If the teacher does not know the answer to a question, others can be asked for suggestions or opinions. In any case, bluffing is not a good solution. It is better to admit not knowing and promise to find out.

Attention seeking (making too long, too frequent or irrelevant comments)

The teacher may need to request to finish what she is saying first. When listening, the body language can be used to indicate urgency (e.g., by looking at the clock), the student may be directly reminded that time is limited or asked to let others contribute ('Let's hear what others think . . .'). If an irrelevant comment is made, it is important to try to find in this comment something that is connected to the actual topic and use it to return to the point. If the issue is wrong timing, the teacher can acknowledge that the comment is valid and suggest returning to it later on, when a relevant subject is addressed.

Non-co-operation (e.g., refusing to do an exercise) and non-participation

The teacher might need to discuss the reasons for refusing to participate. It may be worth asking the student to try anyway, and see if they feel the same after. The teacher can also ask others if it is OK that one of them is not participating. If they are uncomfortable, the student in question can either turn their back or temporarily leave the room. If a number of students feel uncomfortable doing an exercise, it is probably best to leave it for later. If a student does not participate in a discussion, for example, this may simply be due to shyness. It is important to watch out for any signs that the student wants to communicate, to ask a non-intrusive question now and then, without pushing too hard or too often.

Dealing with sensitive issues

The nature of these classes is such that exceptionally some sensitive issues may be brought up or outward emotional reactions, such as crying, may be experienced. Some teachers might feel out of their depth in this situation, not knowing what to do. The important thing to bear in mind is that, although such experiences may appear hard and even painful, they are rarely harmful and the outcome is frequently beneficial. The other thing to keep in mind is that in these situations it is more important to be with the student involved rather than attempting to do something. This means giving the student time and space to express their emotions, offering sympathy and a sense of safety through body language (e.g. remaining calm); and making sure that other students do not interfere (by, for example, making some unwarranted remarks). If it is deemed that the issue may require further attention, the teacher may suggest to the student, after the session (not in front of others), to see a school counsellor. If counselling is not available, the teacher may want to organize a one-to-one chat.

Let the journey begin

This comprehensive introduction has hopefully served the purpose of boosting both the knowledge and the confidence of educators eager to engage with the well-being lessons. We wish you, the reader, a lot of fun and challenge on the way.

Positive Psychology in Action Lessons Grid

	Unit 1: Positive Self	Unit 2: Positive Body	Unit 3: Positive Emotions	Unit 4: Positive Mindset	Unit 5: Positive Direction	Unit 6: Positive Relationships
Lesson 1	Happy Talk	Image Matters	Understanding Emotions	Fixed or Flexible?	Egg Yourself On	Tonic or Toxic?
Lesson 2	Me, Inc.	Supersize Me!	The Negativity Bias	Hope	Nail, Nag, Nudge	Forgiveness
Lesson 3	My Strengths Portfolio	The Nutrition Quiz	Boost your Positive Emotions!	Creative Problem-Solving	The Flow Zone	Listening and Empathy
Lesson 4	Confident You	Mindfulness for Life	Just for Fun	Money, Money Money!	Big Hairy Goals	Sweet Trading
Lesson 5	My Best Possible Self	Go to Bed, Sleepyhead!	Surprising, Spontaneous Savouring!	The Tyranny of Choice	Five Little Pigs	Kindness and Gratitude
Lesson 6	The Strengths Songbook	The Power of Exercise	Mental Time Travelling	Think Yourself Happier	The Balancing Act	Happiness across Cultures

UNIT 1: POSITIVE SELF

Lesson 1: Happy Talk

LESSON PLAN

Aims and Objectives	Resources
To be able to define happiness To discuss the scientist's definitions To understand the importance of happiness To judge a personal level of happiness	PowerPoint Lesson 1 Post-it notes Happiness Quotes handout How Happy Am I? handout Happiness Detective handout

Teacher Explanation: Reflecting on Happiness (10 min.)
Teacher-led Discussion and Reflective Questioning

● Students to define happiness and explain when they are happy.

● Students to record their answers on Post-it notes (in one or two words).

Class Activity 1: In the Eyes of the Wise (10 min.)

Small Group Activity

● In small groups of 5–6, students discuss the different happiness quotes from different philosophers and writers on the Happiness Quotes handout.

● Quotes to be summarized on Post-it notes.

Main Body 1: What Is Happiness? (15 min.)
PowerPoint Presentation and Questionnaires

● Teacher to introduce two scientific conceptions of happiness and well-being: feeling good and flourishing.

● Teacher to explain that feeling good is about having fun; having positive relationships; being healthy and engaging in positive self-talk. Flourishing is achieved through having goals and making a difference to other people.

● Students to position their completed notes on the two corresponding flipchart sheets (feeling good and flourishing).

Class Activity 2: How Happy Am I? (10 min.)
Questionnaire Completion and Scoring

● Students complete and score the Happiness Questionnaire on the How Happy Am I? handout.

Main Body 2: The Importance of Happiness (10 min.)
PowerPoint Presentation and Reflective Questioning

● Teacher to lead discussion on the importance of happiness.

● Teacher to introduce scientific findings, drawing on the nuns study in more detail.

Summary and Homework (5 min.)
Teacher's Instructions

Students to ask at least five people about what happiness is and record the answers on the handout provided.

To download the student handouts and the PowerPoint slides for the lesson, please go to www.openup.co.uk/positivepsychology.

HOW TO

Teacher Explanation: Reflecting on Happiness (10 min.)

Teacher-led Discussion and Reflective Questioning

Many people agree that happiness is what makes life worth living. Ever since time began, humans have indulged in pleasurable activities and searched for lasting contentment. Today, the picture is the same. The pursuit of happiness seems to be readily embraced by the majority and is valued more than the pursuit of money, goodness or going to heaven (King and Napa 1998). In fact, in the past 30 years happiness has received more attention than ever before. There are several reasons why this may be the case:

- First of all, Western countries (like England, France, Germany and America) have achieved a sufficient level of affluence, so that survival is no longer a central factor in people's lives. Quality of life is becoming more important than having money.

- Personal happiness is becoming more and more important because people are becoming more individualistic. This means they worry more about what they think and how they feel, and less about what other people think about them.

- Finally, we now have a science of well-being that aims to study what does and does not contribute to happiness, and how to make things that already work well even better.

> For an excellent summary of the research contributing to the resurgence of happiness studies, *The Psychology of Happiness* by Michael Argyle (2001) is a good introduction.

However, even though we now have a science of well-being, happiness still means many different things to different people. Teacher to ask students what happiness means to them; specifically (a) what does it feel like to be happy? And (b) what are you doing when you feel happy? After discussing some of the answers, students to record their responses in one or two words on Post-it notes and keep them on their desks for the time being.

> Teacher is likely to encounter a diverse range of answers. Many of them will be about being with one's family and friends, just feeling good, a fuzzy sensation, peace of mind, not worrying, etc. British research shows that the most frequently cited categories are relationships; health; contentment; security; personal achievements; and concern for others.

Class Activity 1: In the Eyes of the Wise (10 min.)
Small Group Activity

The pursuit of happiness was debated by the greatest philosophers and is even enshrined in the American Declaration of Independence.

Teacher to ask students to split into small groups and give each group a selection of quotes from philosophers, writers, scholars and other thinkers to discuss. Students to summarize each quote on a Post-it note in one or two words. For example, if the quote is: 'Happiness is not a matter of destination, but a matter of travelling', the summary might be 'travelling' or 'journey'. Each student should have no more than two quotes to summarize. The completed Post-it notes should also be left on their desks for the time being.

Small selections of quotes are provided in the Happiness Quotes handout, but for more quotes, the following websites are a useful source:

http://www.wisdomquotes.com/cat_happiness.html

http://www.quotegarden.com/happiness.html

http://www.heartquotes.net/Happiness.html

http://thehappinessshow.com/HappinessQuotes.htm

Main Body 1: What is Happiness? (15 min.)
PowerPoint Presentation and Questionnaires

Psychology and philosophy recognize two major ideas of happiness and well-being: feeling good (or *hedonic* well-being) and flourishing (or *eudaimonic* well-being). *Feeling good* is what we usually understand as happiness, it means experiencing good emotions and pleasure, engaging in fun pursuits, having good relationships and enjoying life in general. *Flourishing* is an idea that came from Aristotle who believed that just feeling good is not enough for happiness; one also needs to live a good life to be truly happy. So flourishing is about leading a life that appears good not only in one's own but also other people's eyes. Both ideas of happiness are important as together they make our lives more balanced.

The scientific concept of 'feeling good' is summarized in the book, *Feeling Good: The Science of Well-Being* (Cloninger 2004).

Feeling good (or hedonic well-being) is about positive experiences (having fun and positive feelings), positive mindset (using one's thinking to challenge negative thoughts), positive relationships (friends and family) and positive energy (feeling fit, healthy and looking after one's body).

Flourishing (or eudaimonic well-being) is about developing oneself, setting and achieving individual goals (positive direction) and also making a difference to other people.

> Teacher to use own judgement to decide whether or not to introduce the more scientific terms to students.

Students to place their Post-it notes onto the two flipchart sheets, corresponding to both perspectives of well-being. If students need help to sort the statements out, everything concerning experiences (e.g., 'fun') and relationships (e.g., 'my family') will go on the first sheet, while anything related to achievement, aspirations and helping will go on the second.

Class Activity 2: How Happy Am I? (10 min.)
Questionnaire Completion and Scoring

Students to complete the 'How Happy Am I?' questionnaire. Teacher to explain there are no right or wrong answers to the questions asked and there are no wrong or right scores. The scores are there for the students to monitor their own progress, as they will be able to see if their scores have changed or not when they have finished their well-being lessons.

Main Body 2: The Importance of Happiness (10 min.)
PowerPoint Presentation and Reflective Questioning

The common-sense answer to this question is that happiness is good because it feels good. However, research evidence demonstrates that there are other benefits too (Lyubomirsky et al. 2005). (These benefits below are summarized on a PowerPoint slide should you choose to use this.)

Happiness enhances creativity and divergent thinking. It appears that happiness, similarly to positive affect, stimulates playing with new ideas. Research also shows that happy people persist longer at a task that is not very enjoyable in itself (only the happiest employees should be attending boring meetings!), are better at multi-tasking and are more systematic and attentive.

People who are happier tend to work harder and are more likely to succeed. In fact, happier children even tend to earn higher salaries when they grow up (Judge and Hurst 2007).

People who are happy have better friends and relationships, in general, they are more popular, trust people more and also help them more.

What is even more fascinating is that well-being is associated with a long life. Some researchers analysed the application letters of nuns entering convents at the age of 18 for expressions of happiness. All these nuns had a very similar, moderate lifestyle – they didn't smoke or drink, had a good diet and worked as teachers. The results indicated that happiness expressed in these letters at the age of 18 predicted life duration. Years later, at the age of 85, 90 per cent of the nuns whose happiness was in the upper quarter were still alive compared to 34 per cent of those who were least happy. Even at the age of 94, over half (54 per cent) of the happiest nuns were still alive, while only 11 per cent of those whose happiness fell into the lowest quarter were still living. So happiness can buy one an extra 9.4 years of life (Danner et al. 2001)!

Summary and Homework (5 min.)
Teacher's Instructions

Teacher to ask students to take on the role of happiness detectives, using the Happiness Detective handout and find out what happiness is for at least five people they know. Students to record their answers and then allocate them into the feeling good and flourishing categories.

UNIT 1: POSITIVE SELF

Lesson 2: Me, Inc.

LESSON PLAN

Aims and Objectives	Resources
To understand the purpose of creating a personal brand identity (PBI) To create a PBI through the development of a 30-second ad To increase levels of self-confidence	Personal Brand Identity handouts, Parts 1, 2 and 3

Teacher Explanation: Developing a Personal Brand Identity (PBI) (5 min.)
Teacher Presentation

● Teacher to introduce the purpose of the lesson and explain the reasoning behind developing a PBI.

Class Activity 1: My Personal Brand Identity (10 min.)

Individual Activity

● Teacher to download the Personal Brand Identity (PBI) handout and ask students to complete Part 1 only. (Instructions for completion are on the sheets.)

Class Activity 2: First Impressions? (15 min.)

Class Activity

● Students to complete Part 2 of the PBI handout. This means that students need to ask three different people in the classroom two questions and record their answers.

● Students can also ask their teacher to answer their questions.

Class Activity 3: My 30-Second Ad (10 min.)
Individual Activity

● Teacher to hand out the 30-second ad sheet (PBI handout Part 3) and ask students to design their own 30-second ad. Instructions for completion are on the sheets.

Class Activity 4: Sharing My Ad (15 min.)
Classroom Activity

● Students to form small groups of five people, swap ads with someone else and read out that person's ad to the other people in the group.

Summary (5 min.)

Teacher to summarize by reiterating that the purpose of personal branding is for students to gain further clarity about who they are, what they stand for and what is unique about them. It is not about being like someone else or trying to copy someone else's talents or attributes. Research suggests that the more young people learn to like themselves for what they truly are, the greater their levels of personal happiness and the more long-lasting its effects in life.

To download the student handouts and the PowerPoint slides for the lesson, please go to www.openup.co.uk/positivepsychology.

Lesson 2: Me, Inc.

HOW TO

Teacher Explanation: Developing a Personal Brand Identity (PBI) (5 min.)
Teacher Presentation

The aim of this lesson is to help students create a personal brand, so that they learn to become effective in taking charge of their own identity and how they project this to others. A personal brand can be defined as gaining clarity about who you are, what you stand for and what is unique about you. As many students will understand, all successful companies have a great brand image and individuals are no different.

Students will learn that confidence comes from the ability to project the person of today as well as reflecting and dreaming on the kind of person they might want to be. Confidence goes beyond image and good looks and reflects a positive direction in life. In the course of the lesson, students will create their own 30-second advert. In order to do this, students will decide what they believe their identity is and what others think about their identity, design their ad and have it read out to group members.

> A possible YouTube clip to demonstrate how a brand goes beyond looks is the Intel ad. This can be found at: www.youtube.com/watch?v=jqLPHrCQr2I (or type 'Intel Ad – sponsors of tomorrow' into the YouTube search engine).

Class Activity 1: My Personal Brand Identity (10 min.)
Individual Activity

Teacher to hand out the Personal Brand Identity (PBI) handout and ask students to complete Part 1 only. Instructions for completion are on the sheets. The purpose of this first handout is for students to start making conscious decisions as to their personal brand.

> The field of personal branding is best summarized in the accessible book by Mary Spillane, *Branding Yourself* (2000). For general positive psychology inspiration in this area, see *Living Well* (1998) by Mihaly Csikszentmihalyi.

Class Activity 2: First Impressions? (10 min.)
Class Activity

Students to complete Part 2 of the PBI handout, which means asking three different people in the classroom two questions and recording answers. It is worth the teacher checking that students are replying honestly and positively, and the teacher can also help students with their answers.

Class Activity 3: My 30-Second Ad (10 min.)

Individual Activity

The teacher issues Part 3 of the PBI handout – the 30-second ad sheet – and asks students to design their own 30-second ad. Instructions for completion are on the sheets.

Class Activity 4: Sharing My Ad (10 min.)

Classroom Activity

Students to form small groups of five people. The authors recommend that, rather than read out their own 30-second ads, students swap ads with someone else and read out that person's ad to the other people in the group. This is for two reasons. It means the students will have to take the exercise seriously and write something legible on the handout; it will also help the shyer members of the class who find it difficult to talk about themselves openly.

Summary (5 min.)

Teacher to summarize the lesson with a reminder the purpose of personal branding is for students to gain further clarity about who they are, what they stand for and what is unique about them. It is not about being like someone else or trying to copy someone else's talents or attributes. Research suggests that the more young people learn to like themselves for what they truly are, the greater their levels of personal happiness and the more long-lasting its effects in life.

UNIT 1: POSITIVE SELF

Lesson 3: My Strengths Portfolio

LESSON PLAN

Aims and Objectives

To understand what positive psychology means by 'strengths'

To understand the 24 strengths shared across the world

To identify individual high and low strengths

To appreciate other people's strengths

Resources

Approximately six sets of The Strengths Handout

My Strengths Portfolio handout

Same Strength, Different Ways handout

Teacher Explanation: What Are Strengths? (5 min.)
Teacher Discussion

● Teacher to introduce the concept of character strengths and the purpose of this lesson, which is to build a personal strengths portfolio with a series of three activities.

Class Activity 1: Understanding Strengths – Part 1 (15 min.)

Small Group Activity

● Students to form themselves into groups of four and hand each group a pack of strengths.

● Students to lay out the 24 strengths where they can all be seen (floor or desks).

● Students to choose their three highest strengths and share these with the group.

● Students to record these strengths on their individual My Strengths Portfolio handout.

Class Activity 2: Understanding Strengths – Part 2 (15 min.)

Small Group Activity

● Staying in their groups, students to choose their three lowest strengths.

● Students to share these with the group and complete their My Strengths Portfolio handout.

Class Activity 3: Strengths Feedback (15 min.)
Small Group Activity

- Students to form new groups of four people and explain they are going to give strengths feedback to each other.

- Students to choose one strength card per person in the group and give feedback to each individual highlighting the strength and how that person has demonstrated it.

- Students to complete their Strengths Portfolio sheet.

Summary and Homework: Same Strengths Different Ways (10 min.)
Teacher-Led and Whole-Class Discussion

- Teacher to remind students of the importance of knowing their strengths, linked to research.

- Students to use one of their strengths in a different way each day next week (five days), recording the results.

- Students are advised to visit the website, www.viastrengths.org and ask their parents to register them for the student version of the Via Strengths Questionnaire, so that they can compare their online results with those they achieved in class.

To download the student handouts and the PowerPoint slides for the lesson, please go to www.openup.co.uk/positivepsychology.

HOW TO

NB: This lesson works well when run together with Lesson 6, The Strengths Songbook, although they can both be taught independently.

Teacher Explanation: What Are Strengths? (5 min.)

Teacher Discussion

The concept of positive traits, including the recognition and development of strengths, is central to positive psychology. It is a great way for students to start identifying what is good about themselves and what their strengths are. This in turn means they are able to understand why others are different and how this helps us get along with other people. Teacher to show the quote below and ask for students' opinion:

Each of us has much more hidden inside us than we have had a chance to explore.

(Muhammad Yunus)

Students are asked to define the concept of 'strength', with the teacher adding the scientific definition as 'a positive character trait that feels authentic and energising' (Linley 2008). This means that when an individual thinks about their strengths, they should feel a real sense of 'yes, that's me' and positivity ('wow, I love having that strength'). In this lesson, students will be building a 'strengths portfolio', that is, an understanding of their strengths, including their highest and their lowest strengths, as well as gaining feedback from other classmates. The reason for concentrating on strengths over two lessons is due to the abundant research that indicates the link between strengths, performance and life satisfaction.

Strengths are at the very core of positive psychology because they relate to understanding the plus side of the life equation – the presence of psychological health, rather than the absence of psychological illness. The development of positive traits is one of the stated three aims of positive psychology, alongside the development of positive institutions and positive emotions (Seligman 2002).

Doctors and psychiatrists share a common 'bible', the DSM-IV (*Diagnostic and Statistical Manual of Mental Disorders* by the American Psychiatric Association) which provides a manual for measuring what could be wrong with you, by classifying diseases and their symptoms. Peterson and Seligman's book *Character Strengths and Virtues* (2004) is the first ever attempt by psychologists to classify what could be right with you and the strengths of character that enable the good life to be possible.

Class Activity 1: Understanding Strengths – Part 1 (15 min.)

Small Group Activity

Students to form themselves into groups of four and teacher to give each group a set of strengths cards which can be printed out from the handout provided. The 24 strengths are divided (by scholars of positive psychology) under the banners of six virtues and these strengths and virtues are listed below for your information.

> Research indicates that top achievers know their capabilities and set their goals slightly above their current level of performance, whereas low achievers are unaware of their abilities and often set unrealistically high goals. Essentially, high-performing students build their lives around their talents and strengths. They learn to recognize them and develop them further. As far as weaknesses are concerned, they need to be understood, recognized and managed. (Clifton and Anderson 2001)

Strengths of Wisdom and Knowledge

- creativity
- curiosity
- open-mindedness
- love of learning
- perspective (wisdom)

Strengths of Courage

- bravery
- persistence
- integrity
- vitality

Strengths of Humanity

- love
- kindness
- social intelligence

Strengths of Justice

- citizenship
- fairness
- leadership

Strengths of Temperance

- forgiveness and mercy
- humility and modesty
- prudence
- self-regulation

Strengths of Transcendence

- appreciation of beauty and excellence
- gratitude
- hope
- humour
- spirituality.

Students to lay out the 24 strengths where they can all be seen (floor or desks) and to examine them in detail. Each student is to pick out their three highest strengths (it doesn't matter if students choose the same strengths) and share this information with one another.

Students to fill in the first part of their My Strengths Portfolio handout.

> Sets of 24 strengths cards can be ordered from www.positiveinsights.co.uk.

Class Activity 2: Understanding Strengths – Part 2 (15 min.)

Small Group Activity

Strengths psychometrics and literature often concentrate on understanding and using an individual's highest strengths. Yet it is vital for students to realize the importance of developing a broad strengths portfolio that includes recognizing and building capability around their lowest, as well as highest, strengths. Without this, it is possible for students to dismiss the need to recognize and develop the most common low youth strengths such as perseverance, humility and self-control.

For the next exercise, students are to stay in their groups, choose their three lowest strengths and share these with their group. Teacher to ask students to reflect on one of their lowest strengths and consider a couple of simple ways they can start to improve it. For example, if 'self-control' is the lowest strength, students can decide to:

- take two deep breaths before speaking their mind;
- spend just ten minutes more on their homework before doing something else;
- listen to someone more intently, rather than letting their minds wander;
- turn off their computer and tidy their room!

Students to complete their My Strengths Portfolio handout.

> The importance of developing and celebrating strengths among adolescents is highlighted in a 2006 study in which researchers concluded that 'the building and enhancement of competence and character can prevent negative outcomes and are also important outcomes in their own right, indicative of positive development and thriving' (Park and Peterson 2006, p. 892). In this study, four strengths in particular were robustly linked to greater life satisfaction: hope, love, gratitude and zest.
>
> The strength of perseverance appears key to exam success. This was also the conclusion of a longitudinal study of 140 eighth-grade students – 'the findings suggest a major reason students fall short of their intellectual potential: their failure to exercise self-discipline' (Duckworth and Seligman 2005, p. 939).

Class Activity 3: Strengths Feedback (15 min.)
Small Group Activity

Leaving a set of strengths on each table, students are to form new groups of four people and give strengths feedback to each other. Students are asked to choose one strength per person in the group and give feedback to each individual, highlighting the strength and how that person has demonstrated it. It is important the students identify the strength, as well as an example of how they have seen this being used, as research has demonstrated that 'knowledge' together with 'usage' makes for a useful strength.

For example, a student might choose 'kindness' for one of their classmates and then explain how this student was kind to them or to someone else recently and how this specifically helped.

Students to complete the last part of their My Strengths Portfolio handout.

Summary and Homework: Same Strength, Different Ways (10 min.)
Teacher-Led and Whole-Class Discussion

Teacher to remind the students of the importance of knowing their strengths and concurrent research. For homework, students are asked to choose one of their top strengths and over the course of a week, use it in a different way each day, recording the results.

Students can also complete the VIA Strengths Online Questionnaire at home. If students visit the website www.viastrengths.org and ask their parents to register them for the youth version of the VIA Strengths Questionnaire, they can compare their online results with those they achieved in class.

> Their VIA Inventory of Strengths is a self-report questionnaire which can be completed free online. The youth version, suitable for young people aged 10–17, is also available online at the same website address.

UNIT 1: POSITIVE SELF

Lesson 4: Confident You

LESSON PLAN

Aims and Objectives	Resources
To define what confidence is To understand the four sources of confidence To understand their 'sappers' and 'boosters' To use consequential thinking to increase confidence	Juggling or tennis balls Stopwatch The Confidence Quiz handout Consequences handout

Class Activity 1: Great Balls of Fire! (5 min.)
Group Activity

● The class is to form a circle (around the desks if necessary) and follow the instructions for the Great Balls of Fire! exercise.

Teacher Explanation: Defining Confidence (10 min.)
Teacher Discussion

● Students to discuss the strategies used by the class to be successful in the exercise.

● Teacher to explain how these strategies relate to confidence.

● Students understand the definition of confidence.

Class Activity 2: The Confidence Quiz (15 min.)
Individual Activity and Teacher Presentation

● Students complete and assess the Confidence Quiz handout.

● Students understand the four sources of confidence: experience; role models; encouragement; feelings.

● Teacher explains the meaning of 'sappers' and 'boosters'.

Class Activity 3: Personal Boosters (15 min.)
Small Group Activity

● The class forms small groups with approximately six students in each group.

● Each individual tells the group about their positive role model and personal 'booster'.

● Teacher to offer some personal examples so the students fully understand the exercise.

Class Activity 4: Consequences Mind Game (10 min.)
Individual Activity

● Teacher to explain how confidence can be undermined (usually out of fear and/or embarrassment).

● Students to indulge in some 'what if' consequential thinking with the Consequences handout.

Summary (5 min.)

● Teacher to summarize by reminding students that possessing a strong sense of self-confidence (not arrogance) is an essential part of a positive self.

To download the student handouts and the PowerPoint slides for the lesson, please go to www.openup.co.uk/positivepsychology.

HOW TO

The authors recommend starting this lesson immediately with the first activity without an initial introduction. This lesson covers the basics of building confidence (an essential part of a positive self).

Class Activity 1: Great Balls of Fire! (5 min.)
Group Activity

Students are to form one large circle with teacher randomly allocating the students a number from 1 to the maximum number of students in the circle (say, 30). (It is important that the teacher ensures the allocation is random and not side by side.) Explain the rules:

1. Students are now in a 'production line' and have to throw the ball to each other in the circle ensuring that the ball is thrown to sequential numbers. That is, the students must throw the ball from person number 1 to number 2 to number 3, etc.

2. This must happen three times and their time will be recorded on a stopwatch.

3. The ball must be touched by each person and, if is dropped, they must start again.

When concluded the first time, the students are given their time. Students are then informed they have to halve their time and rethink their strategy. (The students can move, change positions, do the exercise differently – but they must ensure the ball touches each person's hand.) After the second completion, these instructions are repeated until students are able to complete the exercise in less than ten seconds. NB: Most teams eventually complete this exercise in approximately five seconds by huddling together and passing the ball over the tops of their hands.

> Great Balls of Fire! is an experiential exercise for students who want to explore their confidence; their ability to solve a problem and to think 'out of the box'. See www.mindspring.uk.com.

Teacher Explanation: Defining Confidence (10 min.)
Class Discussion

Students to suggest the strategies they used in order to successfully complete the exercise with answered recorded on the whiteboard. These should include:

- optimism

- hope

- perseverance
- creativity
- playfulness
- trust
- self-belief
- team-working.

Teacher to explain that these strategies are all hallmarks of a confident person which is the theme of this lesson.

> Confidence is an essential part of developing a positive self. It is central to what we achieve in life, what we believe about ourselves, our trust in others and our ability to achieve our goals (Craig 2007).

What is Confidence?

The students are asked for their own definitions of confidence, which could include any of the following factors:

- being relaxed, comfortable and secure with yourself;
- believing in yourself;
- not believing that someone else is always better;
- doing as well as you can so that doors open in the future;
- setting goals that are not too high so that you can achieve;
- not having a huge gap when comparing yourself to others;
- not compensating for being insecure by acting brashly or aggressively;
- having the ability to act confidently, even though you don't feel it;
- having the self-esteem to fail and make mistakes;
- being comfortable with yourself and not worrying what other people think;
- having the guts to achieve what you want.

A good definition of confidence is:

> The ability to be yourself and to go anywhere and try anything in a positive fashion without fear or embarrassment to yourself or others (Taylor 2003).

> Confidence is a word that is frequently used in everyday language yet there is no single definition of confidence. However, researchers have agreed that confidence focuses on two related ideas: (1) being sure of your own abilities; and (2) having trust in people, plans or the future (Taylor 2003; Craig 2007).

When discussing confidence, the most commonly used terms by psychologists are self-esteem, self-efficacy and optimism. The scientist and confidence researcher Albert Bandura specializes in self-efficacy – an individual's belief that he or she has the skills or knowledge necessary to achieve a particular goal, or could acquire it in the future.

Therefore, holding back on what a person can offer the world or 'hiding one's light under a bushel' is the opposite of confidence. It is also important that the teacher distinguishes confidence from arrogance.

Class Activity 2: The Confidence Quiz (10 min.)

Individual Activity and Teacher Presentation

Students are given the Confidence Quiz and asked to assess their own levels of confidence. After completion, teacher to explain the four sources of confidence (and record on whiteboard).

The Four Sources of Confidence

1. *Experience*: Essentially, the positive achievements a person has already experienced with this activity. For example, if a student has got a good mark in maths, they start to believe that they can do well at maths. If they have played a great game of football and scored a couple of goals, they start to believe they can play football well.

2. *Role models*: Admired people who have the desired skills. The success of these people is motivating, so a person can copy their skills, knowledge and attitude.

3. *Encouragement*: Other people's belief in one's abilities and positive support matters.

4. *Feelings*: Mood and the reaction to stress are what matters here. If a person gets too stressful about doing something new, the activity will be avoided or done badly. Therefore, one of the ways to increase confidence is to learn how to cope better with stress.

Bandura argued that these are four sources of influence on the development of self-efficacy, the closest concept in relation to confidence (Bandura 1997).

Sappers and Boosters

In order to develop confidence, it is evident from the list above that other people have a positive or negative effect on levels of self-esteem and confidence. That is, they will boost or sap levels of energy.

Boosters are those people who are positive, happy and joyful to be around. They can cheer up other people, put zest into a boring lesson and fill the room with can-do vibes that have a ripple effect on everyone else.

Sappers do the opposite. They can put a person down, think negatively, act in a jealous way, drain energy and bring everyone down to their level. This does not mean they are malicious. Often sappers don't realize they are negative and label themselves as 'realists'.

The question a student has to ask is – who boosts, and who drains my levels of confidence and optimism? It is worth students remembering they have the power to choose who to hang around with.

Class Activity 3: Personal Boosters (10 min.)
Small Group Activity

Class to form small groups/circles of approximately six students. Each student is to choose a positive role model and personal 'booster' and relate this to the group. For instance, one of the author's positive role models is her daughter, who is always bouncy and optimistic, and her 'booster' is Chris Evans (the Radio 2 DJ) for his infectious enthusiasm on the radio in the morning!

> It is important for students to be aware of the people who 'sap' their confidence as much as it is to be aware of those who 'boost' their confidence. Young people can be surrounded by others who diminish their confidence, be it family, friends or teachers. An addition to this exercise would be to consider the people and events that sap confidence or negative role models.

Class Activity 4: Consequences Mind Game (10 min.)
Individual Activity

Many young people avoid doing new activities for fear of looking foolish or being humiliated. This is called 'what if?' thinking. That is, worrying about the outcome and fearing for the worst. This last activity is designed to help students face their fears and become more bold and confident. Through asking 'what if?', students imagine the worst, and then they ask 'so what?'. The purpose of the exercise is to help students recognize their ability to cope with any adversity.

Distribute the Consequences handout.

Summary (5 min.)

The lesson can be summarized by reminding students that possessing a strong sense of self-confidence (not arrogance) is an essential part of a positive self.

UNIT 1: POSITIVE SELF

Lesson 5: My Best Possible Self

LESSON PLAN

Aims and Objectives

To understand the importance of a 'Best Self' image

To practise a muscle relaxation technique

To be able to use visualization techniques to enhance their self-confidence and self-esteem

To create a strong image of their 'Best Self'

Resources

My Future Best Self handout

Designing my Future handout

Relaxing music

Teacher Explanation: What Is My Best Possible Self? (10 min.)
Teacher Presentation

- Students are introduced to the concept of Best Possible Self, the research and the benefits of creating a strong, individual and positive self-visualization.

Class Activity 1: Relax Those Muscles! (10 min.)
Whole-Class Activity

- Teacher leads the Progressive Muscle Relaxation (PMR) exercise.

- Teacher leads discussion on the uses of PMR and demonstrates the 'quick fire' technique.

Teacher Explanation: Understanding Visualization (5 min.)
Teacher Presentation

- Students are introduced to the history of visualization.

Class Activity 2: Tapping into the Senses! (10 min.)
Whole-Group Activity

- Teacher leads two visualizations with the class and discusses the outcomes.

Class Activity 3: My Future Best Self (15 min.)

Individual Activity

- Using the handout, students to spend ten minutes writing an initial description that captures their thoughts for their future best self.

- Students to complete a five-minute visualization of their Best-Possible Future Self.

Summary and Homework: Designing My Future (10 min.)

Teacher Instructions

- Teacher to recap on the importance of visualization and the need to practise.

- Given the Best Possible Self concept, students to consider what they can do immediately to make this a reality, recording their thoughts on the handout Designing My Future.

To download the student handouts and the PowerPoint slides for the lesson, please go to www.openup.co.uk/positivepsychology.

Lesson 5: My Best Possible Self

HOW TO

Teacher Explanation: What Is My Best Possible Self? (10 min.)

Teacher Presentation

In this lesson, students are going to explore using the techniques of visualization to create and achieve an optimistic future.

Laura King, a professor at the University of Missouri, pioneered the first-ever systematic experimental study of optimism. She asked participants to visit her laboratory for four consecutive days. On each day they were instructed to spend 20 minutes writing a description of their 'best possible future selves'. This is an exercise in which a person visualizes the best possible future for themselves in all areas of life – home, school, friends, future career, etc., and then captures this in writing. Professor King found that the people who wrote about their visions for 20 minutes per day over several days (relative to those who wrote about other topics) were more likely to show immediate increases in positive moods, be happier several weeks later and even to report fewer illnesses several months on.

> See L. King (2001), 'The health benefits of writing about life goals', for more details.

This exercise was extended by two scientists, Sonya Lyubomirsky and Ken Sheldon, who asked people to continue their writing sessions at home over the next four weeks. Again, participants experienced a significant lift in mood compared to others who simply wrote details of their daily lives – particularly those who applied the exercise with sustained effort.

> See K. M. Sheldon and S. Lyubomirsky (2006), 'How to increase and sustain positive emotion', for more details.

Why did it work so well? Participants found it motivating, relevant to their current lives and easy to relate to. The focus of attention on both the good and the possible produced a burst of inspiration. The combination of writing and visualization is important. People enjoyed visualizing their future goals, but, more importantly, the success of the experiment was due to people building a best possible self *today* that could make that future come true. Teacher to explain that this is the purpose of the lesson – building a best possible self today (with the help of personal visualization) that can make a best possible future come true!

> Researchers studying optimism have also suggested that the reason this exercise works is because optimism is born out of a positive expectation of your future – that is, a belief that your goals can and will be accomplished (Scheier and Carver 1993).

Class Activity 1: Relax Those Muscles! (10 min.)

Whole-Class Activity

Explain to the students that to help them focus their minds, tune out the outside world and relax enough to visualize effectively, you are going to run a Progressive Muscular Relaxation Exercise (PMR) with them. PMR is useful for relaxing your body when your body is tense. The idea is that you tense up a group of muscles so they are as tightly contracted as possible. Hold them in a state of extreme tension for a few seconds. Then, relax the muscles normally. Then, consciously relax the muscles even further so that you are as relaxed as possible. Ask the students to sit somewhere comfortably, close their eyes as you run through parts of the body for them to tense and relax.

> PMR has an excellent historical research base for relieving stress and tension. Two good summaries include a book from Harvard, *The Relaxation Response* (Benson 1998) and a scientific paper by Bernstein and Borkovec (1973).

Here is the most popular recommended sequence for PMR:

- right foot
- entire right leg
- left foot
- entire left leg
- right hand
- entire right arm
- left hand
- entire left arm
- abdomen
- chest
- neck and shoulders
- face.

Teacher to discuss when students might find this exercise useful (for instance, when nervous, scared, anxious or upset) and explain that this exercise can be done in a 'quick fire' way by just tensing the lower limbs, then the chest, then the arms, shoulders and neck – and finally the face.

Teacher Explanation: Understanding Visualization (5 min.)

Teacher Presentation

Before language, the only way humans could think was through images. But as *homo sapiens* became civilized through the increased use of language, the imagery capacity of our brain atrophied. Children reveal considerable ability to visualize but often lose this within a left-brained educational system. However, the right hemisphere, our imagery centre, is fortunately responsive to exercise!

> Leading American psychiatrist John Ratey revolutionized the way of looking at the brain and its ability to create new neural pathways (See his (2003) *A User's Guide to the Brain* for a fascinating and intellectual read!)

Effective visualization is an all-round sensory experience (seeing, feeling and hearing) without the external stimuli – it is imaginary. The experience is a product of memory vividly recalled by reconstructing the image in the mind. Athletes have been using imagery since sport was first conceived, but it has only been used regularly in the last decade, proving to be a key differentiator in a team's success.

> Corbin (1972) and Martens (1982) are sports psychologists who have reviewed the powerful effect of imagery on performance.

Class Activity 2: Tapping into Your Visual Senses! (10 min.)

Whole-Class Activity

Teacher to lead the following two visualizations to stimulate the sensory system:

> Close your eyes, hold your hands out in front of you and imagine you're holding a lemon which you roll between your hands. Bring the lemon up to your nose and smell deeply. Breathe in that smell. Imagine there is a chopping board in front of you. Put the lemon on the chopping board and cut it swiftly in half. Now cut the lemon into quarters. Now pick up one a quarter of the lemon to your mouth and BITE into it – hard.

Teacher to ask students to open their eyes and record whose mouth is full of saliva!

For the second visualization, students are to stand up and close their eyes:

> Imagine you are running for a train. It is a train you urgently need to catch and you can just see it pulling out of the station – RUN! Get your legs pumping; your arms moving and run faster – the train is leaving. At the last minute, you JUMP! And just reach the last carriage...

Students to open their eyes, test their heart rate and record whose heart rate has increased!

> The famous psychologist Dr Luria describes in his (1968) book *The Mind of a Mnemonist* (a person with superior memory) a man who could alter his pulse from a normal rate of 70 beats per minute to 100 beats, then back to 70. He achieved this by seeing himself running after a train that had just begun to pull out and he had to catch up with the last carriage to make it. He reduced his heart rate by imagining himself lying in bed, falling asleep.

Class Activity 3: My Future Best Self (15 min.)

Individual Activity

Using the My Future Best Self handout, students to spend approximately ten minutes gathering their thoughts about life in ten years' time. Writing this down is important as the diary method has been empirically shown to enhance well-being in a sustainable way. Students can equally capture their thoughts visually or in a mind map.

After this, students will experience a five-minute Best Possible Self visualization. Teacher to ask students to sit comfortably, close their eyes and relax their muscles. Ideally, relaxing music will be played:

> Please take five minutes to visualize your best possible self that you have just written about. This means you imagine yourself in ten years' time after everything has gone as well as it possibly could. You have worked hard and achieved what you wanted to at this stage in your life. Think of this as the realization of your potential and imagine what you have studied; what you have achieved; what you will be doing; where you will be living and how you will be feeling about your life.

> For a more detailed explanation of this exercise, see the book, *The How of Happiness* (Lyubomirsky 2007, pp. 100–11).

Summary and Homework: Designing Your Future (5 min.)

Teacher Instructions

The lesson can be concluded by asking students the question: 'What can you start doing now to help this become a reality?' This enables students to write a brief narrative description of small steps they can take in the next three months to start achieving their best possible future.

UNIT 1: POSITIVE SELF

Lesson 6: The Strengths Songbook

LESSON PLAN

Aims and Objectives
To understand the variety of strengths that exists within the classroom in a visual way
To 'tap into' and recognize high and low strengths through the medium of music
To decide ways to increase and improve personal strengths

Resources
Minimum of nine sheets of flipchart paper or blank poster board
CD-shaped handout
CD cut-outs for each pupil
Coloured pens plus bits and bobs for decoration
Cue cards/postcard/Post-its
Internet to play music

Teacher Explanation: The Strengths Songbook (5 min.)

Teacher Discussion

- Teacher to explain to students the purpose of the lesson – to build a giant poster reflecting the class's strengths in the manner of a songbook.

- If Lesson 3, My Strengths Portfolio, has been taught, students to remember their highest (or preferred) strengths for this exercise.

- If Lesson 3, My Strengths Portfolio, has not been taught, students to decide what they believe their best qualities or strengths are.

Class Activity 1: The Songbook Takes Shape (15 min.)

Individual Activity

- Having been handed out the CD cut-out, students to design a CD cover that visually depicts their individual highest strengths.

- Songbook 'designers' are allocated who paste the CD cut-outs onto the poster wall (leaving room for further work).

Class Activity 2: Contents of the Songbook (15 min.)
Small Group Activity

● Students to write down two songs on postcards or cue cards that highlight their strengths. These are written on postcards or cue cards and placed on the wall (or have the songbook designers stay in charge of this).

Class Activity 3: Songbook Credits (15 min.)
Individual Activity

● The 'credit page' for the songbook is designed, with each student writing one 'thank you to . . . who showed me the strength of . . .' credit.

Summary (10 min.)
Teacher-Led/Whole-Class Discussion

● With the songbook completed, students to reflect on the identified, and shared, classroom strengths.

● Students to understand they can tap into their own strengths, and borrow others' strengths through many means, music being a primary one.

● If possible, students to download the music and create a classroom strengths CD.

To download the student handouts and the PowerPoint slides for the lesson, please go to www.openup.co.uk/positivepsychology.

Lesson 6: The Strengths Songbook

HOW TO

Teacher Explanation: The Strengths Songbook (5 min.)

Teacher Discussion

If the previous lesson, My Strengths Portfolio, has been taught, teacher to explain that the purpose of the lesson is to reinforce the class's strengths that were identified in the last lesson and to create a songbook. This is to help students remember what their strengths are, reflect on the whole strengths of the classroom and renew commitments to increase and improve their strengths profile.

Students should write down their highest strengths.

If the previous lesson has not been taught, teacher to explain the purpose of the lesson is to understand the individual and shared strengths held by students in the classroom. It might be useful to give a brief definition of strengths at this stage, that is, 'a positive character trait that feels authentic and energising' (Linley 2008). This means that when a student thinks about their strengths it should feel genuine (a sense of 'yes, that's me') and positive ('wow, I love having that strength').

In order to decide their best qualities and highest strengths, students can engage in brief self-reflection and can also ask each other to help with this decision, by asking, 'What am I like at my best?'

Teacher to explain that the songbook is going to have three parts: different CD covers designed by each student highlighting their individual strengths; songs that reflect those strengths suggested by the students and songbook 'credits' – that is the friend/individual or family member who perhaps shares the strength, has taught them a strength or role-models the strength.

> Understanding strengths through music and movies is a familiar theme in the strengths research. Chris Peterson, one of the founders of positive psychology and author of *A Primer in Positive Psychology* (2006), recommends songs at the end of each chapter to help bring the research to life and aid the reader get in touch with the lessons through a different medium.
>
> In a similar vein, on the dedicated VIA strengths website, see www.viacharacter.org, two leading researchers have suggested movies and songs that bring to life each of the different strengths. Their research is summarized in the paper, '340 ways to use character strengths', located at www.viacharacter.org/practice/exercises (Rashid and Anjum 2005).

Class Activity 1: The Songbook Takes Shape (15 min.)

Individual Activity

After handing out the CD cut-out, students are asked to design a CD cover that would visually depict their own highest strengths (they can choose one or more strengths to visualize, but probably no more than three). The teacher can bring in some CDs if the students are in need of inspiration (or if they haven't seen a CD for some time!).

The CD cut-outs can be pasted onto the poster wall by a couple of allocated songbook 'designers' (room needs be left for further work).

Class Activity 2: Contents of the Songbook (15 min.)
Small Group Activity

On postcards or cue cards, students to write down a couple of songs that highlight each of the strengths they put on the songbook. These should be placed on the wall (or have the songbook designers remain in charge of this). These examples should be fun, relevant and memorable.

> Research indicates that memories associated with music are so strong that even the mere mention of a song's title or a glimpse of the album cover can bring the recollections of a positive emotion flooding back (Kansas State University 2009).
>
> Oliver Sacks, in his haunting book, *Musicophilia* (2007) goes further than this. Introducing his book and on his website, www.musicophilia.com, he suggests that, as music occupies more areas of our brain than language does, humans are indeed a musical species. In his words, 'Music can move us to the heights or depths of emotion. It can persuade us to buy something, or remind us of our first date. It can lift us out of depression when nothing else can. It can get us dancing to its beat.'

Ideally, play some of the songs over the internet as students come up with their ideas.

Some (albeit old-fashioned!) examples of this might be:

Have a Nice Day – Stereophonics (Optimism/Kindness/Zest)
Don't Stop Believing – Journey (Hope)
I'm Gonna Be (500 miles) – The Proclaimers (Perseverance)
Don't Worry, Be Happy! – Bobby McFerrin (Vitality/Zest)
9–5 – Dolly Parton (Self-Control/Self-Discipline)
Fight for This Love – Cheryl Cole (Perseverance)
Thank You for the Music – Abba (Gratitude/Appreciation of beauty!)
I'll Be There for You – The Rembrandts (theme tune from *Friends*) (Kindness/Love/Loyalty)
You're My Best Friend – Queen (Kindness/Love)
Wonderful World – Louis Armstrong/James Morrison (Gratitude)
Sorry Seems to Be the Hardest Word – Elton John (Forgiveness)

Class Activity 3: Songbook Credits (15 min.)
Individual Activity

Every CD has a credit listing with the artist thanking someone who helped them. The purpose of this exercise is to create such a credit list. Students to think of one person who has either been:

● a friend who shares the same strength;

- a family member or teacher who taught them or showed them how to develop the strength;

- a role model who demonstrates the strength.

Students to write their 'credit' either directly on to the songbook or onto a piece of paper/card/Post-it sticker which is then attached to the wall. The authors suggest students write:

Thank you to.............who showed me/helped me/shares with me/role models to me the strength of ....

Summary (10 min.)
Teacher-Led/Whole-Class Discussion

With the songbook completed, students to take time to look at it; to reflect on the identified strengths and to recognize the shared classroom strengths. Teacher can lead a discussion about the contents of the songbook and how music – as our auditory channel – is an important memory and reflection source. It is important for students to understand that not only do they have so many positive strengths – as individuals and as a class – but that there are people around them they can learn from, particularly when they need a strength they lack.

If possible, the class can create the actual CD through downloading the songs onto a CD.

UNIT 2: POSITIVE BODY

Lesson 7: Image Matters

LESSON PLAN

Aims and Objectives

To debate the role of image in today's culture

To understand what counts and what doesn't regarding image

To understand the message of inside-out vs. outside-in thinking

Resources

PowerPoint Lesson 7
The Body Quiz handout

Teacher Explanation: Image Matters (5 min.)

Teacher Discussion

- Teacher to explain the purpose of the lesson which is to encourage discussion around image and teenagers and to examine the science about looking good.

Class Activity 1: Hot or Not? (10 min.)

Class Activity and Teacher PowerPoint

- Show the five celebrity images on the PowerPoint asking students to answer the brief question at the top of the image.

- Encourage discussion around these images.

Class Activity 2: Does Image Matter? (15 min.)

Small Group Debate

- Students to form into small groups of six and debate a topic. Three students must be 'pro' the topic and three students must be 'against' the topic.

- The question is 'Does image matter in today's celebrity-driven world?'

- Students to spend five minutes in preparation, with three points to support their case.

- Debate is enacted for five minutes and at the end each group offers their outcome.

Teacher Explanation: What Counts? – Exploding Image Myths (15 min.)

Teacher Explanation and PowerPoint

- Using the PowerPoint, the four dominant myths surrounding image are explained, linking the science with the previous two classroom discussions.

Class Activity 3: The Body Quiz (5 min.)

Individual Activity

- Students complete the Body Quiz handout which is linked to the conclusion below.

Summary: Inside-out Versus Outside-in (10 min.)

Teacher-led Class Discussion

- The lesson is summarized by explaining the two concepts of Inside-out and Outside-in.

- The benefits of an outside-in approach are discussed, together with five ways to make it more effective.

To download the student handouts and the PowerPoint slides for the lesson, please go to www.openup.co.uk/positivepsychology.

HOW TO

Teacher Explanation: Image Matters (5 min.)

Teacher Discussion

This lesson explores the role that body image has on teenagers and examines the science behind looking good. As such, it is the first lesson in the section of this book on 'Positive Body'.

Class Activity 1: Hot or Not? (10 min.)

Class Activity and Teacher PowerPoint

At the start of the lesson teacher to show the students the five images on the PowerPoint presentation, asking students to answer the questions at the top as to whether the people shown are Hot? Cool? Sexy? Poetic? etc.

- The purpose of the activity is for the students to start examining their views of celebrity/model images and how this might differ for men and women. Information for each of these images is below:

  1. Size zero model. Anorexic and has been ill for five years.

  2. Ronaldhino. World's most famous Brazilian footballer. Labelled as an 'ugly' celebrity, yet admired by boys and girls across the world and has been the 'face' for Nike.

  3. Shane McGowan. Singer and songwriter with The Pogues. Known as Ireland's most poetic songwriter and in NME's list of All-Time Greatest Rock Heroes. Drug and alcohol addict.

  4. Jocelyn Wildenstein. Famous American socialite who has spent $4 million on plastic surgery.

  5. Jack Black. Famous American actor.

Class Activity 2: Does Image Matter? (15 min.)

Small Group Debate

The science behind image and looking good for young people has two parts. While there is a research confirming that being attractive counts in life, there is a more substantial body of research to demonstrate that it is how a person *feels* about themself that counts and the attitude they radiate to others. As teenagers tend to place such a high emphasis on what they look like, this lesson will not concentrate on the former research. For the teacher's

> purposes, it is worth knowing that research demonstrates a bias in life towards physically attractive children, with teachers, friends, strangers and parents judging attractive children as more competent, academically able, socially skilled and emotionally more adjusted (Dion et al. 1974; Langlois et al. 2000).

Teacher to ask the students to form small groups of six in order to debate with each other, the topic: 'Does image matter in today's celebrity-driven world?'

Three students in each group are to be 'pro' the topic and three students are to be 'anti' the topic. Students should spend five minutes in preparation, developing three points to support their case and subsequently enact the debate for 5–10 minutes. At the end of the debate, each group to summarize and relate their outcome.

Teacher Explanation: What Counts? – Exploding Image Myths (15 min.)

Teacher Explanation and PowerPoint

Using the supplied PowerPoint, teacher to explain the four dominant myths surrounding image, linking the science with the previous two classroom discussions and the scientific research.

> The scientific research behind these myths is summarized in Paul Martin's book, *Making Happy People* (2006), in the chapters dedicated to looking good, wealth and celebrity.

Myth No. 1 – It's What You Look Like That Counts

Wrong. It is how a person *feels* that counts. Excessive narcissism is bad for any person. Research has shown that individuals who place an unusually high value on their own appearance, and who have a strong desire to be regarded as attractive, tend to have poorer mental and physical health than those whose desires are less cosmetically oriented.

This is because body image is psychological in nature. It is influenced by an individual's self-esteem, self-worth, perception of one's body and how others may perceive it. It is not based on the truth, but on the perception of the truth.

Body image is forever changing. It is sensitive to mood swings, physical environment and experiences. It is formed out of every experience and relationships – parents, role models, the media and peers who give a person an idea of what it is like to value the body.

Therefore, body image is not only what a person sees when they look in the mirror, but also what they feel when they think about their body and how they feel in their body. For example, if someone feels ashamed, self-conscious and anxious about their body, they have a negative body image. Equally, if a person feels comfortable and confident in their body, they have a positive body image.

Myth No. 2 – If I Look Like My Friends, I'll Be Happy

Wrong. What is known by the scientists as 'social comparison' is one of the quickest ways to lower self-esteem and damage self-confidence. People with an inherent tendency to judge what they look like (and live like) compared with others can remain dissatisfied with their lot throughout their lives.

> Lyubomirsky (2007) has documented substantial research on the effects of social comparison and Kasser and Ryan (1993) explored the effects of the pursuit of fame as a goal.

Myth No. 3 – If I'm Beautiful, Rich And Famous, I'll Be Happy

Wrong. Sorry, but the pursuit of fame is more often a recipe for unhappiness. Research has found that children whose main aspirations in life centre round money, fame and physical appearance tend to have poorer mental health than those who pursue goals such as developing close relationships or helping others. People who hanker after looking good and being recognized have higher levels of depression and anxiety and experience more physical symptoms such as headaches, lack of energy and lack of vitality.

Myth No. 4 – Girls Care About Their Image More Than Boys

Wrong. Girls *talk* about their image, and other people's images, more than boys, yet on their own boys have been shown to be more vulnerable about their looks than girls. The media and health agencies are reporting that body-image issues have been becoming more and more of a problem for teenage boys over the past decade. This is because boys are increasingly interested in their appearance including their hair, clothes and physique. According to a study done in Australia, it was estimated that about 45 per cent of Western men are unhappy with their bodies to some degree, compared with only 15 per cent some 25 years ago.

> Lina Ricciardelli, of Deakin University in Australia, specializes in researching boys and their image (e.g. Ricciardelli 1999).

Class Activity 3: The Body Quiz (5 min.)
Individual Activity

Students to complete the Body Quiz handout, which contains ten self-explanatory questions regarding body and self- image. The quiz can be used to link to the summary below.

Summary: Inside-out Versus Outside-in (10 min.)
Teacher-led Class Discussion

The lesson can be summarized by briefly explaining the two concepts of Inside-out and Outside-in. An *inside-out* person is obsessed by their own problems and anxieties with no time for anyone else. For the most part, they don't mean to be like this, but their lack of confidence has made them self-preoccupied. An *Outside-in* person is more interested in other people than in themselves. The five ways to become more *outside-in* are summarized on the final PowerPoint slide, or can be put on the whiteboard. They are as follows:

1. Make it your mission to put other people at their ease.

2. Get them to talk by asking questions and build on their answers with further questions.

3. Seek out common interests or similarities so that the other person can relax with you.

4. Face them straight on so you can see their reaction and they can see yours. Smile encouragingly at them when they are talking to you.

5. Practise this as often as possible when you meet other people for the first time. You will then have no time to worry about your own lack of confidence and, as a result, you will be more confident yourself!

> The concepts of Inside-out versus Outside-in have been summarized by Ros Taylor in her book *The Ultimate Book of Confidence Tricks* (2003). Her work is based on the learning previously documented in Lessons 2 and 4 (Me, Inc. and Confident You).

UNIT 2: POSITIVE BODY

Lesson 8: Supersize Me!

LESSON PLAN

Aims and Objectives	Resources
To relate exercise to kilojoules calories expended To understand how different types of food utilize calories To understand how to maximize their calorie intake and energy levels.	Access to computer lab Calculators Internet access (to show YouTube clip) Fast Food Facts handout

Teacher Explanation: *Supersize Me!* – the Documentary (15 min.)
Teacher Presentation and Internet Presentation

- Teacher to explain the purpose of the lesson and show a clip of the *Supersize Me!* film http://www.youtube.com/watch?v=N2diPZOttyo.

- After the clip, teacher to lead a brief discussion into eating habits.

- Class is split into small groups, given the website for the next exercise and directed to the computer lab (with calculators!).

Class Activity 1a: The Worst You Can Eat! (10 min.)
Small Group Activity

- In the computer lab, students to use the calorie counter and design the *least efficient* menu they can develop for the given calories (2300).

Or

Class Activity 1b: Eating for Health (10 min.)
Small Group Activity

- At the computer lab, students to use the calorie counter and design the *most efficient* menu they can develop for the given calories (2300).

Class Activity 2: Picture Perfect (15 min.)
Small Group Activity

● Students to create a visual poster highlighting their best or worst menu for display.

Summary and Homework: Fast Food Facts (10 min.)
Teacher Instructions

● Students to explore and record on the handout interesting and surprising Fast Food Facts.

To download the student handouts and the PowerPoint slides for the lesson, please go to www.openup.co.uk/positivepsychology.

Lesson 8: Supersize Me!

HOW TO

Teacher Explanation: *Supersize Me!* – the Documentary (15 min.)
Teacher Presentation

Teacher to explain the purpose of the lesson is for students to understand, and make sense of, the link between calorie intake, food and health. The starting point for the lesson is the opening of a (2004) documentary, *Supersize Me*, directed by and starring Morgan Spurlock, an American independent filmmaker. Spurlock's film follows a 30-day time period (February to the beginning of March 2003) during which he limits himself to eating only McDonald's food. The film documents this lifestyle's drastic effects on Spurlock's physical and psychological well-being. During the filming, Spurlock dined at McDonald's restaurants three times per day, sampling every item on the chain's menu at least once. He also 'super-sized' his meal every time he was asked. Spurlock consumed an average of 5000 calories (the equivalent of 9.26 Big Macs) per day during the experiment. As a result, the then-32-year-old Spurlock gained $24\frac{1}{2}$ lbs ($1\frac{3}{4}$ stone, 11.1 kg), a 13 per cent body mass increase, and experienced mood swings, sexual dysfunction and liver damage. It took Spurlock 14 months to lose the weight he gained.

A good 7-minute edit of the film can be found here (or type 'Supersize me in 7 mins' into YouTube) http://www.youtube.com/watch?v=N2diPZOttyo.

After the clip, teacher to lead a brief discussion as to the attraction of fast food for some people and how healthy the students believe their eating habits to be.

> At Linkoping University, scientist Fredrik Nyström repeated the experiment under laboratory conditions, raising the calorie intake by fast food to 6000 kcal per day for seven of his students. The results of the experiment were different than those in Spurlock's film. While the students gained 5–15 per cent extra weight during the study, and complained of feeling 'tired and bloated', no mood swings were observed. 'Significant' changes in the participants' livers were, however, observed. Nyström ultimately decided that individual variations in metabolism could have a massive effect on a subject's response to such a diet.

Teacher to divide the class into small groups and explain the following:

Imagine you have walked your 10,000 steps vigorously today and, in doing so, burned up 300 calories (www.eatwell.gov.uk). Given that the normal recommended calorie intake is approximately 2000 calories per person per day (this varies with gender, height, weight and age but is a good estimate), this means that today you can eat 2300 calories (to maintain your existing weight).

Using a calorie counter on the internet, students are going to devise two different menus for efficient and inefficient calorie burning. Teams can be given either Activity 1a (the worst menu) or Activity 1b (the best menu)(or both).

Class Activity 1a: The Worst You Can Eat! (10 min.)
Small Group Activity

In the computer room students are given the website address of the calorie-counting website, www.weightlossresources.co.uk/calories/calorie_counter.htm and asked to use the calorie counter to design the least efficient menu possible for one day for the given calories (2300).

For example, a person could eat 2300 calories by consuming the following:

100g bar of milk chocolate for breakfast	525 calories
Egg fried rice and Chinese balls for lunch	530 calories
Cheeseburger and fries for supper	809 calories
125g of sweet popcorn for snack	505 calories
Total	**2369 calories**

Only allow the menu to contain one item of any foodstuff (i.e. not five Mars bars).

Class Activity 1b: Eating for Health (10 min.)
Small Group Activity

Ask the other half of the class, using the same website, to use the calorie counter and design the most efficient menu possible for one day for the given calories (2300).

Class Activity 2: Picture Perfect (15 min.)
Small Group Activity

Back in the classroom, students are asked to transform their recommendations for the rest of the class using visuals to demonstrate what is on the menu. Students can be challenged to think about how a company might want the consumer to view the menus that you have devised. Can they make the menus look appetising so that fellow classmates might actually want to eat the things on it?

Summary and Homework: Fast Food Facts (10 min.)
Teacher Instructions

Using the internet or other means, students are asked to record on the Fast Food Facts handout facts about the fast food industry that they find interesting and surprising. For instance, students might like to explore how much fast food is eaten around the world; why people are attracted to fast food; the most popular fast food and how much the industry is worth.

> For instance, McDonald's has approximately 55 million customers each day worldwide, with 22 per cent of the customer base eating there once a day, so-called super-heavy users.

UNIT 2: POSITIVE BODY

Lesson 9: The Nutrition Quiz

LESSON PLAN

Aims and Objectives	Resources
To pool their knowledge about nutrition to answer the quiz and extend previous learning To increase knowledge of nutrition	PowerPoint Nutrition Quiz – lesson 9 PowerPoint Quiz Answers – lesson 9 Nutrition Quiz Answer Sheet Bells/clackers per team Eating Well handout

Teacher Explanation: Setting up the Quiz (10 min.)

Teacher Presentation

- Teacher to divide the class into teams of four or five people and introduce the Nutrition Quiz.

- Team should decide on a name and be given a bell or 'clacker' as their team 'noise'.

- Teams are given their Nutrition Quiz answer sheets.

Class Activity 1: The Nutrition Quiz (20 min.)

Whole-Group Activity and PowerPoint Presentation

- Teacher to run the Nutrition Quiz (without answers).

Class Activity 2: The Nutrition Quiz Answers (20 min.)

Whole-Group Activity

- Teams to swap Nutrition Quiz answer sheets as teacher leads class through the answers and obtains final team scores.

Summary and Homework: Eating Well (10 min.)

Teacher Instructions

- Teacher to discuss with the students the questions they didn't know and the answers that surprised them. Depending on which areas of the quiz the students got wrong (or which areas fascinate them), students are to research the website, www.eatwell.gov.uk, and write a paragraph on an area about food and nutrition that is of interest on the handout provided.

To download the student handouts and the PowerPoint slides for the lesson, please go to www.openup.co.uk/positivepsychology.

Lesson 9: The Nutrition Quiz

HOW TO

Teacher Explanation: Setting up the Quiz (10 min.)
Teacher Presentation

Teacher to download and print about seven copies of the Nutrition Quiz answer sheet and explain to the class they will be doing a nutrition quiz to test their knowledge. The class should be divided into teams of 4–5 people and each team is to give themselves a team 'name' and choose a bell or clacker as their team noise (in our experience, this helps control the running of a quiz!). Teams may only answer a question if they have sounded their team 'noise', with the first team to make a noise given the initial opportunity to answer the question. Five points per correct answer are available (with bonus points available at the teacher's discretion!).

Class Activity 1: The Nutrition Quiz (20 min.)
Whole-Group Activity and PowerPoint Presentation

To run the quiz, the PowerPoint needs to be on full screen. Then, in a similar way to the BBC's *A Question of Sport* (if seen!), a team chooses their preferred number. When the teacher clicks on this screen, the question comes up. Each team has 30 seconds to answer the question (it is useful to have a visible countdown timer for this – or a designated timekeeper). Teacher should not give answers at this stage.

Class Activity 2: The Nutrition Quiz Answers (20 min.)
Whole-Group Activity

Teams to swap Nutrition Quiz answer sheets and teacher to run through the answers. Bonus points are awarded at the teacher's discretion with final team scores on the whiteboard.

Summary and Homework: Eating Well (10 min.)
Class Discussion

Teacher to lead a discussion with the students about the quiz, including unknown and surprising answers. Depending on which areas of the quiz students got wrong (or which areas fascinate them), students are asked to research the website, www.eatwell.gov.uk and write a paragraph on an area about food and nutrition that interests them.

UNIT 2: POSITIVE BODY

Lesson 10: Mindfulness for Life

LESSON PLAN

Aims and Objectives	Resources
To understand what mindfulness means To relate to the importance and benefits of being present To practise some simple mindfulness techniques	Pen and paper A Mindful Week handout Ideally a large room

Teacher Explanation: What Is Mindfulness? (10 min.)
Teacher-led Discussion

● Teacher to introduce the concept of mindfulness, the science and the benefits of practice. An outline of the four exercises will be introduced.

Class Activity 1: Learning to Focus (10 min.)
Individual Activity

● With pencil and paper, students are asked to choose an object (or person) in the classroom, to focus their attention on a small detail and draw this object.

Class Activity 2: The Body Scan (10 min.)
Teacher-led Class Practice

● Teacher to lead the Body Scan mindfulness exercise.

Class Activity 3: Walking Mindfulness (10 min.)
Teacher-led Class Practice

● Students are introduced to the concept of walking mindfulness and led through the exercise.

Class Activity 4: The Bubble Sensation (10 min.)

Teacher-led Class Practice

- Students discuss the uses of mindfulness in observing thoughts and emotions and led through the 'bubble' exercise.

Summary and Homework: Putting it into Practice (10 min.)

Teacher Explanation

- The lesson is summarized through discussing the different meditation techniques.

- Students are asked to practise being present over the course of a week using A Mindful Week handout and notice what happens.

To download the student handouts and the PowerPoint slides for the lesson, please go to www.openup.co.uk/positivepsychology.

Lesson 10: Mindfulness for Life

HOW TO

Teacher Explanation: What Is Mindfulness? (10 min.)

Teacher-led Discussion

Teacher introduces the notion of mindfulness. Mindfulness is about paying attention to oneself and the things around you in a particular way. This is done on purpose, in the present moment (the now) and without judgement (not seeing things as good or bad).

Teacher to ask students if they have ever had the sensation of completing a journey and forgetting parts of it; not remembering what they ate for breakfast that morning; blanks in conversations; forgetting if they washed their hair in the shower, etc. This is because days are spent being very busy, running around and doing a lot of things. So much so, it is common not to notice what is actually being done. Equally, people's minds are constantly busy with lots of chatter going on: things to remember, people to text, email or call, online conversations to have, homework, things to be done. There are routines at home and at school, and people go through the motions, not truly paying attention to what they are doing, minds wandering elsewhere, and so people can end up eating without tasting, looking without seeing, and talking without knowing what they are saying.

Teacher to ask students to stop for a moment and reflect on the following questions:

> Have you been paying attention to the room you are in? What is the temperature? How does it smell? What are you sitting on? Is it comfortable? And your body: Do you have any aches or pains? Are your muscles tight or relaxed? Is your stomach pleasantly full or is it painfully empty?

Students will start to understand the many stimuli surrounding them in their immediate environment, sensations in their body, and thoughts and feelings in their mind which they were probably not consciously aware of.

> Mindfulness is defined as 'the awareness that emerges through paying attention on purpose, in the present moment, and nonjudgmentally to the unfolding of experiences moment by moment' (Kabat-Zinn 2003, p. 145). The first part of this definition expresses the idea that mindfulness is an active process; it involves active attention which leads to awareness. The second part of the definition highlights that it regards the present, rather than the past or future. The third part emphasizes that the attention is non-judgemental and accepting, without thinking that the experience of the present moment is good or bad, right or wrong, important or not.

Mindfulness can help everyone become more present, so life can be experienced in the here and now.

> Research into mindfulness interventions with adolescents (Greco et al. 2005; Semple et al. 2006) shows that cultivating mindfulness leads to:
>
> - reduced stress, anxiety, worry and depression;
> - improved sleep and capacity for relaxation;
> - greater self-awareness;
> - less reactivity, anger and frustration;
> - increased self-confidence;
> - enhanced relationships with peers, teachers and parents;
> - greater capacity for focus and concentration;
> - better learning outcomes;
> - greater levels of enjoyment in life, in self-reports and reports by parents and teachers.

NB: For information, mindfulness should not be confused with meditation. The goal is not to achieve a higher state of consciousness or to distance oneself from the present experience, but rather to have an increased awareness of the present moment. Mindfulness can be practised through meditation, but unlike these other techniques, mindfulness can also be practised through such activities as mindful eating, mindful drawing or mindful walking (Dimidjian and Linehan 2003).

In teaching mindfulness to students, it is important to start with success, so starting simply is better. The exercises here will progress from concrete attention to the environment, then moving to the experience of the body, and finally, introducing attention to the mind and meditation exercises (Hooker and Fodor 2008).

> Mindfulness forms a substantial part of two clinical programmes: Mindfulness-Based Stress Reduction (MBSR) and Mindfulness-Based Cognitive Therapy (MBCT). They include simple breathing techniques, body scans and yoga stretches to help participants become more aware of the now, including getting in touch with moment-to-moment changes in the mind and the body. Both programmes are highly effective in preventing recurrent depression and have also been used for other disorders such as stress, anxiety, chronic pain, etc. (Segal et al. 2002; Baer 2003). There is also considerable research demonstrating the effectiveness of mindfulness for healthy participants (Brown and Ryan 2003).

Class Activity 1: Learning to Focus (10 min.)
Individual Activity

With pen and paper to hand students are asked to select an object to draw. Examples of objects might be a phone, a shoe, scissors, or a clock. In starting to draw, students need to be reminded that the activity is not about their ability to draw, but the ability to focus attention on smaller and smaller details. Teacher to lead a discussion with students about the experience of spending time really looking at an object that might otherwise have been something they never took time to notice.

Class Activity 2: The Body Scan (10 min.)

Teacher-led Class Practice

The key objective in doing the body scan is to enhance awareness of physiological sensations and to train one's mind to stay focused over a longer period of time on a particular task in the now. Students are asked to lie down on the floor (space permitting) or to sit upright on their chairs. Teacher to explain that during the exercise they will be asked to focus for a while on the movement of their breath before directing their attention to each region of their body and observing what happens when doing this. It is important they do it with an open mind, curiosity and a sense of adventure.

> The 'body scan' is frequently used in mind/body therapies such as yoga, meditation, biofeedback, T'ai chi, Qi gong, body psychotherapy, etc. (Carmody and Baer 2008).

Here is a brief version of the Body Scan:

Lying down now ... Breathe in s-l-o-w-l-y and deeply through your nose. Feel your abdomen move outwards as your diaphragm contracts and draws air into your lungs. Your chest should not rise noticeably.

While breathing slowly, direct attention to your left foot. Feel your foot. Curl your toes once to fix your awareness to it. Now relax ...

As you breathe in through your nostrils, slowly scan your left leg from foot to knee, and up through your thigh.

As you breathe out, trace your leg down to your foot. Do this three times, then take your mind off your breath and remain with your foot.

Feel the sensations in your foot. Simply become aware of them. Scan your left lower leg. Accept any tension or discomfort. Scan slowly, up through your thigh now.

If thoughts appear, that's fine. Gently come back to your breath, and shift awareness over to your right foot.

Slowly inhale while scanning through your right calf, knee, and thigh ... Exhale and scan back down. S-l-o-w-l-y. Now let go of your breath and remain with your foot.

Scan for any sensation in your foot ... calf ... Thigh ... Simply accept all sensations and feel what happens. Relax ...

Now focus on your stomach. Feel it r-i-s-i-n-g as you breathe in. Sinking as you exhale. Nice and slow. Your heart probably slows down. This is normal. Remain aware of your stomach, your breath ... up and down. Become aware of sensations. Relax ...

Now follow the same procedure with your left hand and arm as you did with your leg. You may clench your fist at first to really direct your awareness to your left hand. Breathe ...

Now scan up along the length of your arm, to your chest. Then down your right arm to your right hand. Remain there. Breathe. Sense and scan. Relax ...

Come back up to your chest. Continue scanning up along your neck and to your face. Gently clench your jaws and release. Feel the sensations in your jaws, your throat. Breathe and scan. Feel how the back of your head rests against the floor.

Scan the top of your head. Relax ...

Now detach from all body parts. Breathe ... Feel how everything is connected, resting gently on the floor. Just breathe, let any sensation come to you. Accept it as a part of you. Return to your breathing. Just breathe for a minute and feel your body. Then sit up slowly.

Reproduced with kind permission from www.meditation-techniques-for-happiness.com.

Class Activity 3: Walking Mindfulness (10 min.)
Teacher-led Class Practice

The purpose of the Walking Mindfulness exercise is to bring attention to the body and how the student physically interacts with the environment. Effectively this is mindfulness in action, with the experience of walking being used as the focus. The exercise can be done easily with a group of students together, however, it is important that it be done in a room large enough for everyone to move around without being obstructed by many objects or being too crowded, so that they may remain focused on their own experience. Students may also enjoy doing this with music playing in the background.

Students are asked to move around the room as softly as they can, as if walking on eggshells or on a delicate glass floor. Awareness of each movement made is important, for example, feeling the thigh muscle lift the leg and move it to next position, feeling the foot coming off the floor and setting it back down, feeling their hands and arms in space. Students might move faster or more slowly at times. They might focus on their left leg for a few steps, then focus on the right leg. If students' thoughts begin to wander away from their body and their experience of moving, they should note what they were thinking about, and return their attention to a part of their body (adapted from Fontana and Slack 1997).

Class Activity 4: In a Bubble (10 min.)
Teacher-led Class Practice

After the last exercise, students should find a seat again and relax their minds by becoming aware of their breath. Teacher to remind students that the purpose of mindfulness is to understand they are the producers of their thoughts which come and go and influence their feelings and actions. One exercise to enhance awareness of how they are the producers of their own thoughts is the following:

> To focus on awareness of the thinking process as well as letting go and not engaging thoughts, the meditation of the bubble is a useful mindfulness technique (LeShan 1974). The aim of this practice is to slow down, observe thoughts, and release them or let go without judgement.

Teacher to begin by reading the following script slowly and in a calm voice. Then, allow the students to continue the meditation for a few minutes in silence, setting his or her own pace. This meditation can also be adapted to feature thoughts on clouds drifting across the sky:

Begin by sitting in a comfortable position, with your back straight and shoulders relaxed. Softly close your eyes. Imagine bubbles slowly rising up in front of you. Each bubble contains a thought, feeling, or perception. See the first bubble rise up. What is inside? See the thought, observe it, and watch it slowly float away. Try not to judge, evaluate, or think about it more deeply. Once it has floated out of sight, watch the next bubble appear. What is inside? Observe it, and watch it slowly float away. If your mind goes blank, then watch the bubble rise up with 'blank' inside and slowly float away.

Summary and Homework: Putting it into Practice (10 min.)

Teacher Explanation

Teacher to lead a discussion on the different mindfulness exercises. The authors suggest asking the following questions: Which exercises did they enjoy? Were there any they found hard or easy? How useful do they think mindfulness is? How do they believe they can incorporate it into their daily lives?

> The good news is that very new research suggests that effective meditation practice is as simple as focusing on your breath. Dobkin and Zhao (2011) compared the effectiveness of various practices used in a mindfulness-based stress reduction programme for people who had medical treatment for breast cancer or other chronic illnesses such as depression, anxiety and bowel inflammation. Not only was awareness of breath perceived to be the most useful, but it was also most effective in reducing symptoms of stress.

For homework, students are asked to practise mindfulness consciously over the period of a week, with one specific practice each day, using A Mindful Week handout. This could be just awareness of breathing; walking mindfully to school; eating deliberately; paying close attention to a friend's conversation; or focused attention on schoolwork.

UNIT 2: POSITIVE BODY

Lesson 11: Go to Bed, Sleepyhead!

LESSON PLAN

Aims and Objectives	Resources
To understand the purpose and benefits of sleep To develop their knowledge about sleep To understand the consequences of not getting enough sleep To develop strategies for waking up well and achieving quality sleep time	PowerPoint Lesson 11 PowerPoint Sleep Myths Sleep Diary

Teacher Explanation: The Purpose of Sleep (5 min.)
Teacher Presentation and Internet Presentation

- Teacher to explain the purpose of the lesson and introduce the quiz.

Class Activity 1: 15 Sleep Myths – Fact or Fiction? (15 min.)

Whole-Class Activity and PowerPoint Presentation

- The class is divided into smaller teams and the teacher runs the Sleep Myths quiz (on PowerPoint).

- Class discussion on the quiz.

Teacher Explanation: The Brain, Sleep and Science (10 min.)
Teacher PowerPoint Presentation

- Using the PowerPoint presentation (Brain, Sleep and Science Facts) teacher to explore with the students:

  - what is sleep and what happens when you sleep;

  - the purpose of sleep;

  - the consequences of not getting enough sleep.

Class Activity 2: Strategies for Getting to Sleep (10 min.)
Paired Activity

● Students to discuss, in pairs, as many strategies as possible for getting to sleep (and at least one strategy for waking up!) as possible.

Teacher Explanation: The Science behind the Strategies (15 min.)
Teacher Discussion and PowerPoint Presentation

● Students' answers to be compared with suggested strategies in the PowerPoint presentation.

Summary and Homework: Sleep Diary (5 min.)

● Students to fill in a sleep diary over the next week and report back next lesson.

To download the student handouts and the PowerPoint slides for the lesson, please go to www.openup.co.uk/positivepsychology.

HOW TO

Teacher Explanation: The Purpose of Sleep (5 min.)

Teacher Presentation

An introduction to sleep:

> All things considered, sleeping is pretty creepy. For a third of your life you're just not there, floating in this suspended state, everything slowed down. Except, at points, your brain is more active than when you're awake, and it's consolidating memories from the day and solving problems for you. And then sometimes you dream; you walk or talk in your sleep. Or drool. Weird. What's going on here?

> This introduction to sleep is taken from the acclaimed scientific guide to sleep and stress, *Why Zebras Don't Get Ulcers* (Zapolsky 2004, p. 227).

Teacher to briefly introduce the importance of sleep, particularly for adolescents, and explain that human beings are believed to be the only species on earth to resist the pull of sleep. Humans can see sleep not as a physical need, but a statement of character, with resistance of sleep often viewed as a sign of strength!

> An excellent meta-analysis of sleep research for children is contained in the paper by Sadeh, Raviv and Gruber (2000).

Research now indicates that adolescents are suffering from what is called 'the lost hour', that is, they are staying up later and having to get up earlier for school. The consequence is sleep deprivation on a massive scale. Therefore, in this lesson, the students will be exploring what sleep is; what it is for; the importance of sleep; the consequences of not getting enough sleep; and some strategies for getting to sleep.

> Scientist David Dinges (2007) did a series of experiments on shortening people's sleep to 6 hours a night. After two weeks they proved to be as impaired as someone who has stayed up for 24 hours straight.

Class Activity 1: 15 Sleep Myths – Fact or Fiction? (15 min.)

Whole-Class Activity and PowerPoint Presentation

To start off the exploration of sleep, students are going to do a quiz, Sleep Myths – Fact or Fiction? The quiz, including all the answers and explanations, is on the PowerPoint.

> The quiz is adapted from information from the National Sleep Foundation (NSF). The NSF is an independent, evidence-based, non-profit organization dedicated to improving public health and safety by achieving understanding of sleep and sleep disorders, and by supporting sleep-related education, research, and advocacy. To find out more, look at www.sleepfoundation.org.

The class is divided into small teams with pen and paper. There are 15 questions in the quiz and students have to answer 'Fact' or 'Fiction' to each question. The authors suggest awarding 5 points for the correct answer and a further 10 points available for a good explanation of the answer. Team scores should be recorded on the whiteboard.

NB: The answers and explanations to each question are on the individual slides, so care should be taken when running the quiz to put it on full slide show first and then only click through to the answer after the student's answer has been heard.

After the quiz has finished, teacher to discuss with students what they found interesting and/or surprising.

Teacher Explanation: The Brain, Sleep and Science (10 min.)

Teacher PowerPoint Presentation

Using the PowerPoint presentation (Brain, Sleep and Science Facts) teacher to explore with the students the nature of sleep; the purpose of sleep; and the consequences of not getting enough sleep.

Dr Matthew Walker of University of California, Berkeley, explains that, during sleep, the brain shifts what it learned that day to more efficient storage regions of the brain. Each stage of sleep plays a unique role in capturing memories. For example, studying a foreign language requires learning vocabulary, auditory memory of new sounds and motor skills to correctly enunciate new words. Vocabulary is synthesized by the hippocampus early in the night during 'slow-wave sleep', a deep slumber without dreams. The motor skills of enunciation are processed during stage-two sleep and the auditory memories are encoded across all stages. Memories that are emotionally laden get processed during REM sleep. The more a person learned during the day, the more they need to sleep at night.

> Dr Matthew Walker runs the Sleep and Neuro-imaging Laboratory, in the Department of Psychology, University of California, Berkeley. Further information can be found at www.walkerlab.berkeley.edu.
>
> The basics of sleep, the importance of sleep and the consequences of not getting enough sleep are thoroughly documented (with all the appropriate research) in two good books: *Spark!* (Ratey and Hagerman 2008) and *Head Trip* (Warren 2009).

Class Activity 2: Strategies for Getting to Sleep (10 min.)
Paired Activity

In pairs, students to discuss as many strategies as possible for getting to sleep (and at least one strategy for waking up!).

Teacher Explanation: The Science behind the Strategies (15 min.)
 Teacher Discussion and PowerPoint Presentation

Students' answers can be compared with suggested strategies in the PowerPoint presentation. Below is scientific back-up for each of the answers.

> The science behind the strategies comes from a number of sources listed above and additional papers, *Insomnia and Wellbeing* (Hamilton et al. 2007a) and *Sleep and Psychological Well-being* (Hamilton et al. 2007b).

1. *Why should bedrooms be cool?* Because the circadian rhythm system that helps regular sleep cycles is not just light sensitive, it's temperature sensitive.

2. *Why is TV a problem?* Sitting still and vegging out in front of the TV should, theoretically, help a young person unwind. However, the brightness of the screen is the problem. The light can delay the drop in core body temperature and melatonin, thus delaying sleep onset by up to two hours.

3. *Why prioritize sleep?* After a few days of shortened sleep, the brain makes extra stress hormone cortisol. It takes six times as long for this hormone to drop to a level low enough to allow sleep.

4. *Why have sleep routines?* Inconsistent bedtime routines are like homemade jet lag. Staying up three hours later on weekends is equivalent to flying across three time zones every weekend!

5. *Why bother with after-school activities?* Young people who sleep more are involved with more after-school activities. Schools with delayed start times have seen their students sleep more and increase their participation in sport and extra-curricular activities.

6. and 10. *Why reduce your stress?* The most driven students are the most overscheduled – and the most sleep deprived. A motivated student can sacrifice sleep to maintain grades, but pays the price with higher levels of depression and stress.

7, 8, and 9. *Why not eat, drink and study before bedtime?* All these activities suggest to the body and brain that it is time to stay awake, digest food or rev up the brain cells.

Summary and Homework: Sleep Diary (5 min.)
 Teacher Explanation

Students are asked to fill in a sleep diary over the next week and report back next lesson. The aim of the diary is for students to understand how much sleep they get and how this affects them in their life. An example of a sleep diary is available in the resource pages (and available to use) from the National Sleep Foundation.

UNIT 2: POSITIVE BODY

Lesson 12: The Power of Exercise

LESSON PLAN

Aims and Objectives	Resources
To understand the importance of exercise To learn how to calculate their BMI To appreciate the range of activities that can be viewed as exercise	PowerPoint Lesson 12 My Active Week handout Access to computer Two or three weight scales Two or three height measures

Teacher Explanation: The Benefits of Exercise (5 min.)
Teacher-led Discussion

- Teacher to discuss the reasons why it may be good to be active, drawing on students' contributions.

Teacher Explanation: The Science behind the Exercise (10 min.)

Teacher PowerPoint Presentation

- Using the PowerPoint provided, teacher to explain the research establishing the effectiveness of exercise.

Class Activity 1: Calculate Your BMI (20 min.)
Teacher Presentation and Individual Activity

- Using scales, height measures and access to internet, students to calculate their BMI.

Class Activity 2: Creative Exercising (10 min.)
Whole-Class Activity

- Students to brainstorm as many physical activities as possible that may help them to get/stay in shape and to record in a mind map.

Class Activity 3: The Power of Exercising (10 min.)

Individual Activity and PowerPoint Presentation

- Students to vote on the Top 10 exercises that burn the most calories and compare to PowerPoint list.

Summary and Homework: Choose an Activity (5 min.)

Teacher Instructions

- Students are to choose three different activities they would like to try in the next week and record the effect of their activities on My Active Week handout.

To download the student handouts and the PowerPoint slides for the lesson, please go to www.openup.co.uk/positivepsychology.

Lesson 12: The Power of Exercise

HOW TO

Teacher Explanation: The Benefits of Exercise (5 min.)

Teacher-led Discussion

Teacher to discuss with the class the reasons why it is good to be active. These may include, but are not limited to, the following:

- It's a great way to have fun with friends and make new ones.
- It's an opportunity for new skills and challenges.
- It can boost your confidence.
- It can improve your fitness.
- It can make your bones and muscles stronger.
- It can improve your posture.
- It can help you maintain a healthy weight.
- It improves the health of your heart.
- It can help you relax.
- It reduces stress.
- It can help you maintain healthy growth and development.

> Psychological benefits of physical activity and exercise are often overlooked (Saxena et al. 2005). Yet psychological benefits of physical activity include enhanced body image, self-esteem and self-perceptions (Moses et al. 1989); improved sleep patterns (Kubitz et al. 1996); reduced emotional distress and increased well-being (Steptoe et al. 1996); reduced depression (Babyak et al. 2000; Hassmen et al. 2000; Kritz-Silverstein et al. 2001) and anxiety (McDonald and Hodgdon 1991). In addition, physical activity has been reported to have a preventative element in the development of both physical and psychological illness, for example, HIV progression (Arey and Beal 2002).

Teacher Explanation: The Science behind the Exercise (10 min.)

Teacher PowerPoint Presentation

Using the PowerPoint presentation, teacher to outline the main facts on the importance of an active lifestyle and to distinguish between physical activity (things people do every day or active recreation) and sport/exercise (intentional involvement in structured activities). The Chief Medical Officer recommends that young people should achieve a total of no less than 60 minutes of at least moderately intense physical activity each day, five or more days a week.

Exercise has many physical benefits, including a reduction in obesity, cardiovascular disease, coronary heart disease, stroke, diabetes (type 2), high blood pressure, certain cancers and premature death.

Psychological or mental benefits of exercise include: general well-being, better body image and self-esteem, improved general cognitive functioning among older adults, reduced emotional distress, lower anxiety and reduced depression and stress. In addition, exercising brings a 'feel-good factor'. What about when someone becomes depressed? A possible answer would be to send them to a doctor, who would give them some pills to improve their condition.

A famous study by Babyak et al. (2000) compared three groups of depressed patients. The first group was prescribed anti-depressants, the second group aerobic exercise, and the third a combination of the two. Independently of the treatment regime, most of them had improved four months after taking part. Unexpected results came six months down the road, when 38 per cent of those recovered patients from the first group relapsed into depression; 31 per cent of the third, combination, group went back to ill-health, but only 9 per cent of those who only did exercise became depressed again.

Teacher to introduce the concept of Body Mass Index (BMI). BMI is a reliable indicator of body fatness for most children and teens. BMI does not measure body fat directly, but research has shown that BMI correlates to direct measures of body fat. BMI helps assess whether people are at risk for weight-related health problems.

BMI is measured as follows:

$$\text{BMI} = \text{Your weight (kg) divided by your height (metres)}$$

> Note: BMI does not take into account muscle mass. Since muscle weighs more than fat, a person who is extremely sporty, with lots of muscle can be classified as 'overweight or obese'! BMI must therefore be used in context.
> For children and teens, BMI is age- and sex-specific and is often referred to as BMI-for-age.

Class Activity 1: Calculate Your BMI (20 min.)
Individual Activity

Using scales, height measures and access to the internet, students are to calculate their BMI. If the teacher does not have access to scales and height measures, students are asked to estimate their weight and measure each other's height against the wall. (NB: While the authors have found that students of all shapes and sizes have found this exercise interesting, if the teacher is concerned about this exercise, it can be guided through with volunteers.) The BMI can be measured easily with an online BMI tool.

The NHS calculator uses both metric and imperial measures: available at: www.nhs.uk/Tools/Pages/Healthyweightcalculator.aspx?r=1andrtitle=Interactive+tools+-+BMI+tool.

Pure Life Style calculator uses imperial measures only: available at: www.purelifestyle.co.uk/Calculators.aspx?idx=7.

Class Activity 2: Creative Exercising (10 min.)
Small Group Activity

In small groups, students to brainstorm as many different physical activities as possible that may help them to get/stay in shape. Ideas should be as creative as possible (for example: skipping; breakdancing; hula hooping; trampolining; tae kwon do; playing cards!). Students to create a mind map (or a simple list) of their ideas.

> Trost's (2007) review of children and activity is particularly interesting. He concluded that physically active and fit children tend to have better academic achievement. In addition, he concluded that 5–10 minute activity breaks, yoga breaks and breathing breaks are also beneficial.

Class Activity 3: The Power of Exercising (10 min.)
Small Group Activity

Scientists know that different activities are better for calorie-burning than others. Staying in their groups, students are to guess which activities burn the most calories in one hour, creating their own Top 10 List. Teacher to reveal the Top 10 List, using PowerPoint provided or the list below. Each estimate is for 1 hour of exercising:

10. High-impact aerobics = 500+ burned calories

9. Cross-country skiing = 500+ burned calories

8. Racquetball = 500+ burned calories

7. Backpacking = 500+ burned calories

6. Jogging at a speed of at least 5 mph = 500+ burned calories

5. Stair machine = 600+ burned calories

4. Jumping rope = 700+ burned calories

3. Tae Kwon Do = 700+ burned calories

2. Rollerblading = 900+ burned calories

1. Running at a speed of at least 8 mph = 900+ burned calories

> There are many websites that provide tools to encourage an active lifestyle. Some of the best are: www.activelivingresearch.org; www.kidsexercise.co.uk; www.whi.org.uk.

Summary and Homework: My Active Week (5 min.)
Teacher Instructions

Students are to choose a minimum of three activities they would like to engage in over the next week. They can record the effects of this activity on the My Active Week handout.

UNIT 3: POSITIVE EMOTIONS

Lesson 13: Understanding Emotions

LESSON PLAN

Aims and Objectives

To differentiate between positive and negative emotions

To label and notice a range of different emotions

To understand the six universal emotions and their meaning

To understand the happiness ratio for positive and negative emotions

Resources

Post-it notes
Current newspaper article
White tape
Access to YouTube
Real-life Ratios handout

Teacher Explanation: What Is an 'Emotion'? (10 min.)

Teacher-led Discussion

● Students are asked to define the word 'emotion'.

● Teacher to hear answers and offer scientific definition.

● In pairs, students write down *as many* emotions as they can think of, both positive and negative, and put each one separately on a Post-it sticker.

Class Activity 1: The Emotional Thermometer (15 min.)

Group Activity

● Teacher to mark out the emotional thermometer on the floor with white tape.

● Students to place Post-it stickers of emotions appropriately on the thermometer.

● Students discuss the importance of labelling emotions.

● Teacher to explain the six universal emotions and their meaning.

Class Activity 2: The Hoyt Video (15 min.)
Group Activity and Discussion

- Teacher to show class a YouTube clip about Dick Hoyt and his disabled son, Rick. (Type 'Team Hoyt' into YouTube for the 10-min. clip. There are shorter versions.)

- Discuss the range of emotions the group has experienced.

- Teacher explains importance of emotional self-awareness.

Class Activity 3: Find the Ratio! (15 min.)
Small Group Activity

- Teacher to introduce the concept of happiness ratios.

- Students are given a current newspaper article in small groups of 3–4, to record and count positive and negative words and calculate the happiness ratio.

Summary and Homework: Real-life Ratios (5 min.)
Teacher's Instructions

Students to observe a conversation, news item or a movie episode, calculate the ratio of positive to negative words and record in the Real-life Ratio handout.

To download the student handouts and the PowerPoint slides for the lesson, please go to www.openup.co.uk/positivepsychology.

Lesson 13: Understanding Emotions

HOW TO

Teacher Explanation (10 min.)
Teacher-led Discussion

The term 'emotion' is notoriously difficult to define. However, scientists and researchers broadly agree that it is any feeling about a situation, person or object that causes changes in our body and/ or our heads – that is, they cause changes in physiological arousal or cognitions. The reason emotion is so hard to define is that the experience is subjective and therefore is different for every person.

In pairs, teacher to ask students to write down *as many* emotions as they can think of, both positive and negative. Stimulate thinking with examples, such as 'sadness', 'joy', 'anger', 'excitement' and put each one separately on a Post-it note.

Class Activity 1: The Emotional Thermometer (15 min.)
Group Activity

The 'emotional thermometer' should be marked out on the floor with white tape. Using the tape, put a plus sign at the top and a minus sign at the bottom. Mark the centre point with a 'o'. Students to place their Post-it notes of emotions appropriately on the 'thermometer', with strongest positive emotions at the top (i.e. elation), the strongest negative emotions at the bottom (i.e. anger) and mild ones towards the centre (i.e. contentment). Add to the range of emotions if there are only a few. Here is a list to draw on:

Defiant	Worried	Hopeless	Excited	Peaceful
Annoyed	Anxious	Tired	Enthusiastic	Mellow
Fearful	Incensed	Challenged	Proud	Relieved
Angry	Envious	Optimistic	Happy	At ease
Frustrated	Exhausted	Confident	Stimulated	Passive
Impatient	Sad	Engaged	Astonished	Serene
Defensive	Depressed	Receptive	Carefree	
Irritable	Empty	Eager	Calm	

NB: Teacher to ensure this thermometer is large, so that students can walk up and down it during the class session as they discuss different emotions.

> The list of emotions is drawn from work by Loehr and Schwartz (2003) who explored the relationship between energy and emotions and the *The Circumplex of Emotions* (Carr 2004).

Teacher to ask students why we should label or name emotions. Questions to ask include:

● How useful is it to label emotions?

● In what ways does it help you to give it a name?

> The first stage in understanding emotions is to learn to label and recognize emotions. People who are skilled at perceiving emotions in themselves and others have an advantage in social situations; they are more likely to understand things from another person's perspective and are more empathic (Goleman 1996).

● Would the same emotion be expressed in the same way in different countries?

Teacher to explain that there are six universal emotions, and they each have a meaning and purpose:

Emotion	Universal meaning
Fear	Possible threat
Joy	Gain something of value
Sadness	Lose something of value
Anger	Blocked from getting something
Disgust	Rules are violated
Surprise	Something is happening

> We can never know if the label is right as the experience of an emotion is personal and subjective. However, research demonstrates that despite this subjectivity, facial expressions of the above six dominant emotions are universal to human culture and thus biological in origin (Ekman 1999). Ekman later expanded this list to 15 emotions to include more positive emotions.

Class Activity 2: The Hoyt Video (15 min.)
Group Activity and Discussion

Teacher to show a YouTube clip about Dick Hoyt and his disabled son, Rick. The class is asked to think about the range of emotions they experience while watching the video clip. To find the 10-minute clip, type 'Team Hoyt' into YouTube. (There are shorter versions available if less time is available.)

Teacher to lead a discussion on the range of emotions the group has experienced and explain that sometimes it is hard to identify a specific emotion as a range of emotions can be felt in a short space of time which can be both sad and happy. For instance, in the video one might feel sad that the son is so severely disabled but joyful that the father and son have found an elating way to communicate with each other.

Therefore, it is hard to state definitively that an emotion is either positive or negative. However, the more self-aware students become about their emotions, the easier it is to notice and manage their feelings. This will in turn mean students can recognize and understand the feelings of others – a primary requisite for emotional intelligence.

The concept of 'Emotional Intelligence' incorporates four branches, which are: (1) Perceiving emotions; (2) Understanding emotions; (3) Managing emotions; and (4) Using emotions to facilitate thinking. The term was popularized by Daniel Goleman (1996), although it originated from two scientists, John Mayer and Peter Salovey.

Class Activity 3: The Happiness Ratios (15 min.)
Small Group Activity

Researchers have managed to calculate the ideal ratio of positive to negative emotions. It appears that the ratio of 3:1 or above of positive to negative emotions is conducive to positive well-being, while anything below this ratio (e.g. 2:1) is counterproductive in the long run. So it is important to ensure that for every one negative emotion people have at least three positive ones. But beware, too much of a good thing can be dangerous! Experiencing positivity at above 11:1 can have bad effects as well.

The Positivity Ratio has been substantially researched and documented by Barbara Frederickson (2002).

Teacher to hand out a current newspaper article to small groups of 3–4 and ask students to record and count positive and negative words. Students are asked to calculate the 'happiness ratio' within this article. Teacher to lead a group discussion about what this ratio suggests about newspapers and the media.

Summary and Homework: Real-life Ratios (5 min.)
Teacher Instructions

Students need to observe a conversation, news item or a movie episode of their own choice (no longer than 5 minutes), calculate the ratio of positive to negative words, and record their observations in the Real-life Ratios handout.

UNIT 3: POSITIVE EMOTIONS

Lesson 14: The Negativity Bias

LESSON PLAN

Aims and Objectives	Resources
To be aware of the evolutionary basis for negative emotions and the negativity bias To recognize the NUMB process for managing negative feelings To understand and be able to manage 'triggers' To recognize the 'Sticky Path' of negative emotions	List of emotions on cards Footprint handout Recognizing My Triggers handout Noticing My Emotions handout

Teacher Explanation: The Negativity Bias (10 min.)
Teacher Discussion

● Teacher to explain the evolutionary basis of negative emotions and the purpose of negative emotions.

● Students to discuss and recognize where the negativity bias plays out in their lives.

Class Activity 1: Understanding Your Negative Triggers (10 min.)

Teacher-led Discussion

● Teacher to put the negative emotion cards up on the wall and explain about the 'trigger'.

Class Activity 2: Exploring Triggers (15 min.)
Individual Activity

● Students to explore difficult situations and write down three emotions and three triggers on the Recognizing My Triggers handout.

Class Activity 3: The 'Sticky Path' (20 min.)
Small Group Activity

- Teacher to explain the concept of the Sticky Path – the concept that negative emotions stick to one another to become worse.

- Students to form small groups of 4–6 and each group to come up with their own negative scenario.

- The group is to act out this scenario by catastrophizing it and taking it step by step down a sticky path!

Summary and Homework: Noticing Your Emotions! (5 min.)
Teacher's Instructions

- Students are given an elastic band and asked to wear it on their wrist for one day and 'snap' the band each time they think a negative thought. Students to record their findings.

NB: This lesson is enhanced if it is followed by Lesson 15, 'Boost Your Positive Emotions!' so that students understand how to increase their positive emotions.

To download the student handouts and the PowerPoint slides for the lesson, please go to www.openup.co.uk/positivepsychology.

Lesson 14: The Negativity Bias

HOW TO

Teacher Explanation: Understanding Emotions (10 min.)

Teacher Discussion

Negative emotions are an important fact of life. At important moments they serve to remind people that they have faced a loss; a sadness; a regret or been hurt by someone. It is important to recognize the importance of negative emotions (rather than pretend they don't exist or bottle them up) and to learn how they are triggered and how to manage them. Reducing negative feelings – and increasing positive feelings – influence how well-being in life can be positively affected.

The functions of negative emotions have been clear for a while and have been the focus of attention of psychologists for the past 80 years. Negative emotions, like anxiety and anger, are associated with tendencies to act in specific ways, which are adaptive in evolutionary terms, i.e. the fight or flight response. Thus, fear contributes to a tendency to escape and anger to a tendency to attack. If our ancestors were not equipped with such effective emotional tools, our own existence would be doubtful. Moreover, negative emotions seem to narrow behaviour (while running from danger people are unlikely to appreciate a beautiful sunset). Simply speaking, they focus energy on survival. This is fine if there is a lion in the classroom, but not always so for everyday living in the modern world!

> *Why Zebras Don't Get Ulcers* is an excellent scientific and accessible book on our evolutionary legacy (Sapolsky 2004).

For these reasons, there exists a negativity bias – or a tendency to notice bad things, bad events and bad people easily. Examples of the negativity bias include: (1) people can locate an angry face among happy faces more easily than the other way around; (2) people remember a bad day more readily than a good day; (3) negative events spiral out of control and become more negative than positive events can become more positive; (4) people remember negative things said about them more easily than the nice things. However, despite being evolutionarily adaptive, the negativity bias often leads to depression and anxiety.

> The definitive publication on negativity bias in the field of psychology is by Roy Baumeister et al. (2001) and the phenomenon is often referred to by the paper's title: 'Bad is stronger than good.' Baumeister stressed that because people feel mildly positive most of the time, negative feelings were just more 'attention getting'. Another key paper on this bias was published in the same year by Rozin and Royzman, 'Negativity bias, negativity dominance and contagion'.

Teacher to ask the students to discuss in pairs:

● How does the negativity bias play out in your life?

Teacher to get feedback from the students. For example: students might tell their parents what went wrong during the school day rather than what went right; they might focus on a bad mark for a piece of work, even though the rest of their marks were good; they might remember something mean a friend once said, even though the same person has done lots of positive things since.

Class Activity 1: Understanding Your Negative Triggers (10 min.)
Teacher-led Discussion

Teacher to explain that negative feelings can only be intentionally reduced by noticing that they exist and then understanding the reason behind the feelings. (Students will do further work on noticing their emotions for homework.)

In order to do this, the list of negative emotions can be pasted onto separate cards and placed on the wall. Teacher to explain that something causes us to feel this way and this cause is called a 'trigger'.

Class Activity 2: Exploring Triggers (15 min.)
Individual Activity

Students to note down three triggers in the Recognizing My Triggers handout and then to answer three questions:

1. List three negative emotions you have felt this week/month.

2. What was the occasion when you felt this?

3. What was the trigger for the emotion?

Teacher to offer some examples:

● A lesson that leaves you really BORED.

● Mum shouting at you and you feel UPSET.

● A friend calling you names and you feel ANGRY.

● Someone being unkind to one of your friends.

● FRUSTRATION because you can't understand something straight away.

● SAD because a friend is moving away from the area.

● HOPELESS because you've been left out of the sports teams this season.

By identifying their triggers, students are learning to see *causes* for their emotions and thereby understanding why they feel this way.

> The concept of triggers and causes of negative emotions has been researched by scientists for years and recently developed further by Loehr and Schwartz (2003).

Class Activity 3: The 'Sticky Path' (20 min.)

Small Group Activity

Teacher to explain that science shows people respond internally to negative situations with a combination of thinking, emotions and physical responses. That is, people think and feel something with the body responding at the same time. That means a person can think a situation is scary, feel anxious and their legs shake all at the same time! (That's what happens to most adults when they are asked to do a presentation, which research shows they fear more than death!) What science has also shown is that these thoughts, feelings and physical responses become STICKY, that is, they magnify and get worse!

> Cognitive behavioural therapy (CBT) is used to identify the irrational beliefs, thoughts, and feelings that often lead to debilitating negative emotions and behaviours. By identifying what is negative and unhelpful, any distorted thoughts can be consciously replaced by realistic, helpful and positive solutions. CBT explains how our thoughts, feelings and behaviours can interact to result in a so-called downward spiral. This spiral can also lead to depression and anxiety disorders (Stallard 2002).

To demonstrate this, the teacher places five footprints in sequence on the floor (from A4 footprint handout) creating a 'sticky path' (a line of footprints). The teacher then gives an example of a difficult situation to show how each of these thoughts, feelings or responses can magnify and get worse.

For example, taking it step by step, the teacher can demonstrate the following example:

Step 1	I got a low mark in a test.
Step 2	I felt really stupid.
Step 3	I was unable to work at school that day.
Step 4	I cried most of the night.
Step 5	I was so tired, I slept through my alarm and missed the bus for school the next day.

Class to form small groups of four and each group to come up with their own negative scenario. The group is to act out this scenario by taking it step by step down a negative sticky path!

Summary and Homework: Noticing Your Emotions (5 min.)

Teacher's Instructions

The first stage in learning to understand emotions is to notice one's emotions. Students are given an elastic band and asked to wear it on their wrist for one day and 'snap' the band each time they think a negative thought. Ask students to reverse this exercise on a separate day and to record their positive feelings in the Noticing My Emotions handout.

UNIT 3: POSITIVE EMOTIONS

Lesson 15: Boost Your Positive Emotions!

LESSON PLAN

Aims and Objectives	Resources
To learn about the Broaden and Build Theory To understand the ACT mnemonic for positive interventions To be able to intentionally select positive exercises to increase positive emotions (and reduce negative feelings)	PowerPoint presentation Lively rock/dance music Negative celebrity news story Experimentation Time! handout

Teacher Explanation (15 min.)
Teacher-led Reflective Questioning/PowerPoint Lecture

- Teacher to ask students which positive emotions they can name.

- Introduce the four reasons why positive emotions are important using the PowerPoint.

  - Positive emotions help us think better and be more creative.

  - Positive emotions undo negative emotions.

  - Positive emotions make us more resilient.

  - Positive emotions help us build new skills.

Class Activity 1: Boost Your Positive Emotions (10 min.)
Class Discussion

- Teacher to engage students in class discussion as to existing personal techniques for enhancing positive emotions.

- Explain to students they are in control of their emotions and can ACT intentionally.

- Show the ACT (Active, Calming and Thinking techniques) slides and describe each of the three types of intervention (link this with their identified personal techniques).

Class Activity 2: Understanding Positive Interventions (30 min.)

Teacher Explanation/Group Activity

- Teacher to explain and demonstrate an active intervention.

- Teacher to explain and demonstrate a calming intervention.

- Teacher to explain and demonstrate a thinking technique.

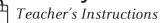

Summary and Homework: Experimentation Time! (5 min.)

Teacher's Instructions

Students are asked to practise one positive intervention each day over the course of a week and to record the effects of each exercise on the Experimentation Time! handout.

To download the student handouts and the PowerPoint slides for the lesson, please go to www.openup.co.uk/positivepsychology.

Lesson 15: Boost Your Positive Emotions!

HOW TO

Teacher Explanation (15 min.)

Teacher-led Reflective Questioning/PowerPoint Lecture

Teacher asks the students to name as many positive emotions and feelings as possible. They are likely to suggest excitement, joy, laughter. Add to these, satisfaction, contentment, fulfilment, pride, serenity and gratitude (sometimes called the emotions of the past), joy, interest, ecstasy, calm, zest, pleasure, flow, ebullience (or emotions of the present), and optimism, hope, faith and trust (emotions of the future).

Consider with the students the purpose of positive emotions and ask the question, 'what good are positive emotions?'

> Given the well-documented evolutionary purpose of negative emotions and the fight/flight syndrome, the question, 'what good are positive emotions?' dominated the early direction of positive psychologists. Barbara Frederickson answered this question in her research (1998), which is presented here in an accessible way for students.

Although positive emotions certainly make us feel good, this, in itself, is not a sufficient answer. In order to stimulate some responses, ask the students to think of a recent situation when they felt really happy and joyful. Ask them what happened before and what happened afterwards. Focusing on what happened afterwards; record on the board some responses consistent with the 'broaden-and-build theory'.

> A lot of other interesting research highlights the benefits of positive emotions. A famous Yearbook Study traced the lives of women who were attending an all-women college in 1965. Their faces were coded for smiling behaviour and those who smiled more genuinely had greater well-being in their later lives. A more worrying study demonstrated that doctors experiencing positive emotions made more accurate diagnoses (Seligman 2002)!

Frederickson demonstrated in her research four reasons why positive emotions are important:

1. *Positive emotions can help us think better and be more creative*: First of all, positive emotions broaden people's attention and thinking, which means that we have more positive thoughts and a greater variety of them. When people are experiencing positive emotions, like joy or interest, they are more likely to be creative, to see more opportunities, to make friends, to play, to be more flexible and open-minded.

2. *Positive emotions undo negative emotions*: It's hard to experience both positive and negative emotions simultaneously; thus a deliberate experience of positive emotions at times when negative emotions take over can serve to undo their lingering effects. Mild joy and contentment can eliminate the stress experienced at a physiological level.

3. *Positive emotions make us more resilient*: Enjoyment, happiness, playfulness, contentment, satisfaction, warm friendship, love, and affection all enhance resilience and the ability to cope, while negative emotions, in contrast, decrease them. Positive emotions can help us do the right thing, help us endure the difficulties and help us find what is good even in negative events, all of which facilitate fast bouncing back after an unpleasant event.

4. *Positive emotions help us build new skills*: Far from having only a momentary effect, positive emotions help to build important physical, intellectual, social and psychological resources that are long-lasting, even though the emotions themselves are temporary. For example, the positive emotions associated with play can build physical abilities and self-mastery, whilst enjoyable times with friends can increase social skills.

Class Activity 1: Boost Your Positive Emotions (10 min.)

Class Discussion

Teacher to ask the students which techniques they currently employ which make them feel better or more positive. Instinctively, the students will already have great methods and the aim of the next part of this lesson is to build on their instincts and offer some more techniques. The important point is to remember that the person is in control – *not* the emotion.

Teacher to show the ACT slides and explain that there are many techniques for managing emotions which we can put under three headings:

ACTIVE ones

CALMING ones

THINKING ones

Class Activity 2: Understanding Positive Interventions (30 min.)

Teacher Explanation/Group Activity

Teacher to show the class the list of active interventions on the PowerPoint and then run the exercise:

● Exercise

● Music

● Dancing

Tell the class you want them each to imagine they are feeling REALLY grumpy. They are in a terrible mood and are going to inflict it on everyone and everything . . . Get them to move around the room adopting a negative physiology (slumped shoulders; slow walking, etc.); the appropriate facial expression; the movement. Ensure they don't speak to each other but walk around the room looking REALLY bad-tempered. Keep this going for a few minutes until everyone is acting the part. Next, put on a loud piece of music and tell the students it is time to shake themselves up; wake themselves up; change their bodies; change their postures and change their facial expressions;

dance; smile; laugh and start to talk to each other. Keep going for a few minutes until everyone is in a good mood.

Explain to the class that movement, exercise, music and dancing are great ways that have been suggested by scientists to get rid of a bad mood and boost an already good mood!

In the past five years neuroscientists have discovered a riveting picture of the biological relationship between the body, the brain and the mind. First, exercise increases the levels of serotonin and dopamine and it unleashes a cascade of neuro-chemicals and growth factors that bolster the brain's infrastructure. The neurons in the brain connect to one another through 'leaves' on tree-like branches and exercise causes those branches to grow and bloom with new buds, thus enhancing the brain function (Zapolsky 2004; Ratey and Hagerman 2008).

Research using brain scanning techniques has revealed that our responses to music are mediated by the same regions of the brain to other pleasurable stimuli, which is why music has been used successfully for many years to help patients suffering from medical conditions (Martin 2006). Internationally renowned author Oliver Sacks goes further than this in his book, *Musicophilia* (2007), by proposing that humans are essentially a musical species.

Teacher to show the students the 'Calming Interventions' slide and explain that 'meditation' is perhaps an off-putting word for a technique and skill that is accessible to everyone. In essence, meditation is simply playing close attention to something, slowing down the activity in the mind and becoming still, quiet and attentive. It helps us to become aware of the here and now when often we are lost in thoughts about the past or the future. It also helps us to become aware of our moods and be less at their mercy and, due to the uplift in positive emotion; it helps us to learn more effectively.

Meditation has been demonstrated to have benefits for health and happiness and recounted in literature from the Buddhist tradition through to the psychological handbooks (Goleman 2003; Ricard 2006). In neuroscience, many controlled lab experiments have now been carried out to show that meditation produces consistent and positive changes in brain activity (Davidson 2003).

Writing down your feelings (also known as the Expressive Writing Paradigm) is also a well-researched method for reducing negative emotion (Pennebaker 1997).

Teacher to lead students through the following visualization:

This visualization is courtesy of Andy Roberts, www.breathe-london.com.

Sit comfortably and close your eyes.

Turning your attention to the area just below your navel – as you breathe in, feel your tummy rising, and as you breathe out, feel your tummy falling.

As you focus on your tummy gently rising and falling with your slow, smooth breath, imagine a beautiful snow-capped mountain . . . and taking on the qualities of strength of the mountain.

[Pause]

Now turn your attention and focus to the area around your chest . . . and below the snow-capped mountain is a beautiful clear blue lake . . . and taking on the qualities of purity, clarity and stillness of the lake.

[Pause]

Now turn your attention and focus to the area just around your forehead . . . and high above the snow-capped mountain and clear blue lake is the deep blue sky. . . and taking on the qualities of freedom and space of the deep blue sky.

[Pause]

So taking on the qualities of strength of the snow-capped mountain . . . the purity, clarity and stillness of the deep, blue lake . . . and the freedom and space of the sky, for the rest of your day.

[Pause]

Very slowly begin making little circles between the tips of your thumbs and fingers . . . and very slowly begin to open your eyes.

> Cognitive techniques for overcoming negative thinking and depressive thoughts are well researched and validated. The Penn Resiliency Programme has established that teaching children resilient thinking patterns has a positive effect on potential depression two years after the programme (Seligman 2002). This will be covered in greater depth in the Part IV Positive Mindset lessons, but it is a good start to introduce children to the concept of 'training' their thinking.

If the teacher has time in this lesson, it is useful to help students learn the technique of 'reframing'. Teacher to explain to the students that the first stage in learning to 'train' their thinking is to ask themselves one simple question: 'What's good about this situation?' In order to do this, the teacher can run the following exercise:

> Split the students into small groups of 4–5. Ask them to read a recent negative news story about a celebrity. Their task is to reframe this story from a positive perspective. The teacher can read the best story to the class.

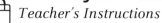

Summary and Homework: Experimentation Time! (5 min.)
Teacher's Instructions

Students are asked to practise one deliberate positive intervention each day over the course of a week and to record the effect of each exercise on the Experimentation Time! handout.

UNIT 3: POSITIVE EMOTIONS

Lesson 16: Just for Fun

LESSON PLAN

Aims and Objectives	Resources
To learn about the different types of humour To appreciate the role of humour To engage in humorous activities	Prize for best joke Humour quotes Digital camera and computer PowerPoint Lesson 16

Teacher Explanation: What's So Funny? (5 min.)
Teacher-led Discussion and Reflective Questioning

● Students to think about their favourite funny story/tale/joke or personal story to share.

● Teacher to discuss with students the purpose of humour.

Main Body 1: All About Humour (10 min.)
PowerPoint Presentation and Reflective Questioning

● Teacher to introduce humour and its meanings.

● Discuss the value of humour and the three major theories of humour.

● After a short PowerPoint introduction to the theories of humour, students are asked to consider humorous situations/jokes/word play based on what they learned (relief, superiority or incongruity theories).

Class Activity 1: Humour Projects (20 min.)
Small Group Activity

● Students are divided into three equal groups to work on one of three different humour projects.

   ● Our portrait: Students play with a digital camera to take funny photos of themselves or others and create a short PowerPoint presentation.

- TV advert: Students create a funny commercial.

- Extraordinary lies: The third group needs to tell extraordinary lies about what they are able to do.

Class Activity 2: Group Demonstrations (15 min.)
Group Performance

- Students to demonstrate their projects, giving 5 minutes maximum per team.

Class Activity 3: Fake it 'Til You Make it (5 min.)
Class Activity

- Teacher to lead the class on a brief laughter session!

Summary and Homework: Just for Fun (5 min.)
Teacher's Instructions

- Find and bring to school a funny photo of themselves or a member of their family.

To download the student handouts and the PowerPoint slides for the lesson, please go to www.openup.co.uk/positivepsychology.

Lesson 16: Just for Fun

HOW TO

Teacher Explanation: What's So Funny? (5 min.)
Teacher-led Discussion and Reflective Questioning

Students are asked to tell the class a joke or favourite funny story (personal or not). The best tale gets a prize (NB: It's a probably a good idea for the teacher to have a couple of jokes of their own to get things started!). Teacher to discuss with the class why it might be good to have fun, laugh and tell jokes (e.g. makes one feel good, helps coping with misfortunes, helps making friends, can help with a boring job, one can come up with new ideas, etc.).

Main Body 1: All About Humour (10 min.)
PowerPoint Lecture and Reflective Questioning

Humour, which is the topic of this lesson, is easier to recognize than to define. The three main meanings of humour include:

- the playful recognition, enjoyment and/or creation of incongruity (that is, laughing at things that surprise us because they seem out of place);

- a composed and cheerful view of adversity that allows one to see its lighter side and thereby sustain a good mood;

- the ability to make others smile or laugh.

Teacher to discuss the fact that humour can be both good and bad, making people feel more uplifted, or worse. Although humour can help us cope or feel better about ourselves, ridicule and sarcasm can be aggressive, as well as self- and other-defeating.

> Humour has many benefits. For example, it is associated with good mood and buffers the effects on mood of life stresses and daily hassles. It increases pain tolerance and even small doses have a positive impact on the immune system. Humour also increases levels of social support through reducing interpersonal conflict and tensions as well as through enhancing positive feelings in others (Martin 2001). It has been estimated that a good laugh produces an increase in heart rate that is equivalent to 10 minutes on a rowing machine or 15 minutes on an exercise bike (Wiseman 2004).

Teacher to introduce the three main theories of humour (McGhee 1999):

- *Relief* – joking allows one to relieve some tension about potentially uncomfortable topics.

- *Superiority* – laughing at someone because of a failing, disadvantage or suffering a small misfortune.

- *Incongruity* – jokes arise out of incongruity between expectations and reality.

> Some interesting facts about humour: People find jokes funniest at 6.03p.m. and least funny at 1.30a.m. (perhaps because they are asleep?!) People also find jokes funniest on the 15th of the month, and less funny towards the end or start of the month. Jokes containing 103 words are the funniest, as are those that reference animals, particularly ducks. So, if you want to make people laugh, tell them a 100-word joke about a duck on the 15th of the month, at 6.03 in the evening . . . (www.laughlab.co.uk).
> LaughLab has some excellent jokes that can be used to illustrate different theories.

After a short introduction to the theories of humour, students are asked to create humorous situations/jokes/word play based on what they have learned (relief, superiority or incongruity theories).

Class Activity 1: Humour Projects (20 min.)
Small Group Activity

Students are divided into three equal groups to work on the different humour projects. In order to allocate students into groups, teacher can ask questions such as: 'Who is good with a digital camera and PowerPoint?', 'Who is good at acting and making stories?', and 'Who is good at lying?'

The first group works on the project entitled *Our Portrait:* Students use a digital camera to take funny photos of themselves or others and create a short humorous PowerPoint presentation of their group or class.

Working on a *TV Advert*, the second group will create a funny commercial. Their task is to use all members of the group and act out this commercial.

The third groups works on *Extraordinary Lies*. The students need to try to tell extraordinary lies about what they are able to do.

Class Activity 2: Group Demonstrations (15 min.)
Group Performance

Each group is to share its achievements with the class, with a maximum of 5 minutes for each demonstration. Enthusiasm is encouraged at the end of each one! When the students perform, it is worth the teacher leading a brief discussion about what was funny (or not) about each performance.

Class Activity 3: Fake it 'Til You Make it (5 min.)
Class Activity

Just as studies show the positive effects of smiling occur whether the smile is fake or real, faked laughter also provides the benefits mentioned. The body cannot distinguish between 'fake' laughter that you just start doing on purpose, and 'real' laughter that comes from true humour – the physical benefits are exactly the same, and the former usually leads to the latter anyway.

Teacher is to lead the class into one big laughing session. Let the class know what is going to happen – they are going to hear a joke and respond with wild laughing – fake or real. Watch the infectious ripple of laughter spread across the class!

Here's an example of a joke that can be used: The second funniest joke out of over 40,000 submitted to the www.LaughLab.co.uk (teacher can judge if they want to use the winner!).

> Sherlock Holmes and Dr Watson were going camping. They pitched their tent under the stars and went to sleep. Some time in the middle of the night Holmes woke Watson up and said: 'Watson, look up at the sky and tell me what you see.' Watson replied: 'I see millions and millions of stars.' Holmes said: 'And what do you deduce from that?' Watson replied: 'Well, if there are millions of stars, and if even a few of those have planets, it's quite likely there are some planets like earth out there. And if there are a few planets like earth out there, there might also be life.' And Holmes said: 'Watson, you idiot, it means that somebody stole our tent.'

Summary and Homework: Just for Fun (5 min.)
Teacher's Instructions

Students are asked to find and bring into school a funny photo of themselves or a member of their family.

UNIT 3: POSITIVE EMOTIONS

Lesson 17: Surprising, Spontaneous Savouring!

LESSON PLAN

Aims and Objectives	Resources
To learn the importance of savouring To understand their personal savouring habits To practise some savouring techniques	Calm music Personal Savouring Questionnaire handout Raisins/fruit per pupil Internet access Get Savouring handout Savouring My Life handout

Teacher Explanation: What is Savouring ? (10 min.)
Teacher-led Discussion and YouTube

- Teacher to run a brief savouring exercise and introduce the topic by defining savouring.

- To get students in the mood teacher can show Cadbury Creme Egg Ad: www.youtube.com/watch?v=olF-KP4J4ew.

Class Activity 1: Personal Savouring Questionnaire (15 min.)
Questionnaire Completion and Scoring with Class Discussion

- Students to fill in the Personal Savouring Questionnaire and discuss answers.

- Teacher to explain the past, present and future dimensions of savouring.

Class Activity 2: Savouring Exercise (10 min.)
Class Activity and Discussion

- Following instructions in the guide, students to intentionally savour food.

- Teacher to lead a savouring discussion about enjoyments and distractions.

Class Activity 3: The Perfect Menu (10 min.)
Paired Activity

- In pairs, students are to design the 'perfect menu' that they would really enjoy savouring! (If possible, these menus could link in with an ICT lesson and be completed on the computer).

Class Activity 4: Increasing Your Savouring Habits (10 min.)

Class Discussion and Personal Activity

- Teacher to discuss with students the rationale behind savouring. Being able to savour allows students to fully experience and enjoy life's pleasures and increase the number of pleasurable experiences in their lives.

- Students to think of, and record, what else they could savour in their lives.

Summary and Homework: Savouring My Life (5 min.)
Teacher's Instructions

- Students to choose two experiences they wish to savour and record the experience on the Savouring My Life handout.

- If possible, students could also make their designed menu at home!

To download the student handouts and the PowerPoint slides for the lesson, please go to www.openup.co.uk/positivepsychology.

HOW TO

Teacher Explanation: What is Savouring? (10 min.)

Teacher-led Discussion and YouTube

As soon as the students come in to class, they are asked to sit, be perfectly still and close their eyes. Teacher to play some calming music in the background until the students quieten down. Ask students to listen to their surroundings, first, concentrating on the noises inside the room and then to the noises outside the room. Students to listen intentionally, playing close attention to everything they hear surrounding them.

As students open their eyes, teacher to explain that today's lesson is about *savouring*, that is, deliberately attending to and appreciating the positive experiences in one's life. That is, to stop for a moment and really enjoy what is going on, allowing oneself get totally immersed in an activity and using all the senses fully.

To get students in the mood, teacher can show the Cadbury Creme Egg Ad: www.youtube .com/watch?v=olF-KP4J4ew.

> Researchers define savouring as any thoughts or behaviours capable of 'generating, intensifying and prolonging enjoyment' (Bryant and Veroff 2006). The ability to savour the positive experiences in life is one of the most important ingredients of happiness and is believed to foster positive emotions and increase well-being (Seligman 2002).

Class Activity 1: Personal Savouring Questionnaire (15 min.)

Questionnaire Completion and Scoring with Class Discussion

Students are asked to fill in the Personal Savouring Questionnaire handout. Teacher to discuss their answers, using questions such as:

- How often do you stop and savour enjoyable activities?

- How or when do you do it?

- What stops us savouring?

- Why do we just gobble down our food?

- Why do we not just stop and stare and take in our surroundings?

- Why do we have to make this deliberate?

Savouring has a past, present and future component. The *past* can be savoured by thinking about all the good things that have already happened in life. For instance, early childhood; past pets; great holidays; fun times spent with grandparents; good friends at primary school.

The *present* can be savoured by truly living in it – eating food slowly and with relish; getting immersed in a book or a movie; truly listening to a friend; getting involved in a project; basking in a friend's accomplishments.

Finally, the *future* can be savoured by anticipating future events and getting excited about them. This is akin to optimistic thinking – thinking the best of a future event.

The Personal Savouring Questionnaire is adapted from 'The Personal Savouring Survey' (Reivich et al. 2007) and the Savouring Beliefs Inventory (Bryant 2003).

Fred Bryant and Joseph Veroff (2006) were the first to study and describe the phenomenon of savouring. In one set of studies, participants were invited to take a few minutes once a day to truly relish something that they usually hurry through (a meal; a shower; a walk). When it was over, they were instructed to write down in what ways they had experienced the event differently and how this felt. In a further study, healthy students were asked to savour two pleasurable experiences a day by reflecting on each for two to three minutes and trying to make the pleasure last as long as possible. In all the studies, participants prompted to practise savouring showed significant increases in happiness and reductions in depression (Seligman et al. 2006).

Class Activity 2: Savouring Exercise (10 min.)
Class Activity and Discussion

In order to intentionally savour some food, students are each given a raisin (or piece of fruit, grapes, blackberries, or raspberries are good) and asked to hold it in their fingers with their eyes closed. Students are to feel the object slowly, smell the fruit and then to put it in their mouths. Instruct students not to bite until they have fully explored the fruit with their mouth, tongue and teeth. Finally, students are to bite into the fruit and notice the flavour in their mouths before swallowing.

Teacher to lead the discussion by asking students what they experienced (with answers captured on the whiteboard):

- What did they notice?

- What specific sensations were they aware of?

- What did they notice about the raisin/fruit that they have never thought of before?

- Ask students about distractions – were they able to concentrate on the exercise?

- What distracted them and why?

- Did they enjoy the exercise and did the process of savouring come naturally?

Class Activity 3: The Perfect Menu (10 min.)
Paired Activity

In pairs, students are to design the 'perfect menu' they would really enjoy savouring. (If possible, these menus could link in with an ICT lesson and be completed on the computer.) This does not have to be a 'sensible' or nutritionally balanced menu! It is about thinking about foods they would really enjoy (future savouring) and anticipating the pleasure of eating them.

Class Activity 4: Increasing Your Savouring Habits (10 min.)

Class Discussion and Personal Activity

Teacher to discuss with students the rationale behind savouring: Being able to savour allows people to more fully experience and enjoy life's pleasures and increase the number of pleasurable experiences available in life. Students to note on the attached handout a list of what else they could savour in their lives, and teacher can encourage students to think about past, present and future events. Here are some ideas:

● a hug with a parent;

● a beautiful day;

● a walk with the dog;

● playing a sport;

● a holiday you had that you loved;

● eating a favourite food;

● listening to a great piece of music;

● past and present friendships;

● an exciting future event.

Summary and Homework: Savouring My Life (5 min.)

Teacher's Instructions

Students are to choose two experiences from the list they wish to savour and then to record the experience on the Savouring My Life handout. It should be stressed to the students that this exercise is not just about *doing* the assignment, but about *enjoying* and *savouring* the experience. Therefore, students should record full sensory details as well as any positive emotions experienced doing the exercise.

If possible, students could also make their designed menu at home!

UNIT 3: POSITIVE EMOTIONS

Lesson 18: Mental Time Travelling

LESSON PLAN

Aims and Objectives	Resources
To understand the meaning and use of positive reminiscence To be able to use three different reminiscence strategies To capitalize on a recent positive experience To enhance a positive experience with visual objects	Access to internet and YouTube Poster paper Share with Me handout

Teacher Explanation: Remember, Remember (15 min.)
Teacher-led Discussion/YouTube clip

- Teacher to start the lesson by taking the students back in time with a clip from an old film that will bring back memories for the students.

- Teacher to discuss the meaning of positive reminiscence and outline the three different reminiscence strategies:

  - positive mental time travel;

  - capitalizing with someone else;

  - capturing memorabilia/objects of interest.

Class Activity 1: Positive Mental Time Travel (10 min.)
Individual Activity

- Teacher to guide the students through a vivid mental recollection of a positive past experience.

Class Activity 2: Share with Me (15 min.)
Small Group Activity

- Students to form pairs and share, in turns, their positive experience with a partner.

- The partner will ask further questions in order to deepen the positive experience.

Class Activity 3: Making it Visual (15 min.)
Individual Activity

- Students to plan the creation of a visual piece of art that captures a positive moment in time or period of time.

Summary and Homework: Developing the Visual Reminiscence (5 min.)
Teacher's Instructions

Students to finish their positive reminiscence artwork at home, adding physical objects (including photos, poetry, pictures, objects).

To download the student handouts and the PowerPoint slides for the lesson, please go to www.openup.co.uk/positivepsychology.

Lesson 18: Mental Time Travelling

HOW TO

Teacher Explanation: Remember, Remember (15 min.)
Teacher-led Discussion/YouTube clip

The aim of this lesson is to help students learn strategies for positive reminiscence, a significant factor for well-being in life. Before discussing the meaning of this and in order to get students in the mood of positively looking back, the teacher can start the lesson by taking the students back in time with a clip from an old film that will bring back positive (or funny, thoughtful, interesting, playful) memories for the students. Depending on the age of the students (ideally you want a clip of something they are likely to have watched when they were 3–7 years old). Clips the authors have used include *The Teletubbies*, a Disney movie, *Bob the Builder*, or *Scooby Doo*.

Teacher to discuss the meaning of positive reminiscence with students and why they think it is important in life. Explain to the students that everyone has personal experiences with positive reminiscence. We can think of a time when we dusted off our photo album and marvelled at how wonderful a holiday was, or when we smiled looking at a hard-won trophy from a sports competition. Past success and emotional high points are a great source of positive emotional energy. Positive reminiscence is a way of engaging with fulfilling memories.

Teacher to brainstorm different ways of remembering good events and experiences. These include diaries, poetry, photos, pictures and personal artefacts.

> Simply speaking, positive reminiscence is the ability to remember past events, situations or people fondly. The advantage of reminiscing has good empirical support. Researchers have found that the ability to transport yourself at will to a different time and place can provide pleasure and solace when an individual needs it most. There is further evidence to suggest positive reminiscence may help to maintain a sense of identity as children grow and mature (Lyubomirsky 2007).

Teacher to explain to the students the three different reminiscence strategies that have been researched and that the students are going to explore all three in this lesson:

1. positive mental time travel (thinking about a past event);

2. capitalizing (sharing that event with someone else);

3. capturing memorabilia/objects of interest that reflect the event.

Class Activity 1: Positive Mental Time Travel (10 min.)
Individual Activity

Teacher to explain to the students they are going to transport themselves to another place and time, just using their imaginations. Explain this is a skill that can be honed with practice. First, ask the students to make a brief list of some positive memories. If students do not know where to start, the teacher can offer suggestions such as going out with friends; playing with pets; a specific holiday they enjoyed or visiting their grandparents. Then ask the class to do the following:

> First, turn to your list of positive memories and choose one to reflect on. Then sitting down, take a deep breath, relax, close your eyes and begin to think about the memory. Allow images related to the memory to come to mind and try to picture the events. If there were people there, think about the people, what they were wearing, what they were saying. Listen to the sounds surrounding you and make them as vivid as possible. Remember where you were and what made this so special. Allow yourself for a moment to be in the luxury of this moment in time.

> This positive reminiscence is based on the research study of Bryant, Smart and King (2005). In the study, people were successfully taught how to travel to a mental destination through recall of positive images and memories. Those participants who reminisced on a regular basis showed considerable increases in happiness, and the more vivid the memories conjured, the greater gain in happy feelings (Lyubormirsky 2007).
>
> Similarly, Lyubomirsky et al.'s studies (2006) show that analysing one's past does little to enhance happiness, while replaying or reliving positive life events as though rewinding a videotape enhances joy and well-being.

Class Activity 2: Share with Me (15 min.)
Small Group Activity

Teacher to explain to the students that visual imagery is one way of positively reminiscing, but scientists have found that our positive experiences are deepened, and subsequently our well-being enhanced, when such experiences are shared with someone else. Explain to the students this is called capitalization. Students are asked to form pairs and share, in turns, their positive experience with a partner. The partner will ask further questions in order to magnify the positive experience. In order to help the partner ask questions, the Share with Me handout can be given to students.

> One of the main savouring strategies is sharing one's positive experiences with others (Bryant and Veroff 2006).

Class Activity 3: Making it Visual (15 min.)
Individual Activity

Having imagined a moment in time, shared it with someone else, students are asked to explore the third aspect of positive reminiscence – bringing the memory to life through visual objects.

Teacher to introduce the notion of personal artefacts – or objects and places that have become symbolically important to us in our personal lives. They can be photographs of special people or places, a special object someone gave to us or made for us, a card or a letter, something we have made, or just something that reminds us of a special time: a ticket stub, a seashell, a rock or a souvenir.

Teacher to explain to students they are going to create a visual piece of art that captures a positive moment in time or period of time. This can be the same memory they have been discussing in the last exercise or a different one.

Summary and Homework: Developing the Visual Reminiscence (5 min.)

Teacher's Instructions

Students to finish their positive reminiscence artwork at home, adding physical objects (including photos, poetry, pictures, objects) and bring it back to school the following week.

UNIT 4: POSITIVE MINDSET

Lesson 19: Fixed or Flexible?

LESSON PLAN

Aims and Objectives	Resources
To understand the difference between fixed and growth mindsets To understand how mindsets affect our goals and efforts	Good at/Bad at handout Impossible or Possible handout PowerPoint Lesson 19

Class Activity 1: Good at/Bad at (10 min.)

Individual Activity and Class Discussion

- As students come in, they write up to five things they are good at and five things they are bad at. Discussing the possibility of changing these leads to a personal identification with the concepts of mindsets.

Teacher Explanation: Mindsets (15 min.)

Teacher PowerPoint Presentation and Class Discussion

- Using a presentation, teacher introduces the notion of mindsets, highlighting the following points: (1) there are two mindsets that people adopt: *fixed* and *flexible*. People can change by choosing to adopt a growth mindset; (2) the brain can and does change too; (3) mindsets affect the goals people pursue, the effort they invest, and the way they deal with failure.

Class Activity 2: Possible or Impossible? (15 min.)

Small Group and Whole-Class Activity

- Students discuss six statements of whether certain achievements are possible or impossible.

- The same discussion is continued with the whole group, with teacher presenting some real-life examples of success.

Class Activity 3: Message from the Past (10 min.)

Individual Activity

- Students are instructed to write a short card to a person next to them about how abilities can be developed, with examples of how they themselves have dealt with some difficulties in the past.

Class Activity 4: If Anything Was Possible (5 min.)
Paired Activity

● Teacher asks students to tell a person next to them five things they would like to learn.

Summary and Homework (5 min.)
Teacher Instructions

● Students are asked to identify a hero and research their accomplishments.

To download the student handouts and the PowerPoint slides for the lesson, please go to www.openup.co.uk/positivepsychology.

Lesson 19: Fixed or Flexible?

HOW TO

Class Activity 1: Good at/Bad at (10 min.)
Individual Activity and Class Discussion

As children come in, teacher asks them to complete the Good at/Bad at handout, indicating up to five things they are good at and bad at. Next, they are faced with a PowerPoint slide, asking them to consider their responses:

- Have a look at your 'Good at' list:
  - Can you get better at it?
  - Do you believe that you are always going to be good at these things?
  - What would happen if you 'failed' at this?
- Have a look at your 'Bad at' list:
  - Has it always been this way?
  - Do you believe you can get better at this?

If students believe that what they are good at and bad at cannot change, they have a fixed mindset. If they believe that with a bit of effort what they are not good at can change and that they can stretch themselves further, they have a flexible mindset. So what is mindset all about and why does it matter?

Teacher Explanation: Mindsets (15 min.)
Teacher PowerPoint Presentation and Class Discussion

During this presentation there are three points that the teacher should aim to get across. The first is that there are two mindsets which people adopt: *fixed* and *growth*. Second, the brain can and does change too. Third, mindsets affect our goals, efforts and meaning of failure.

Teacher begins by challenging the notion that people are 'Born, not made'. It is useful to begin with the question 'Do you think we are born smart?' This allows the teacher to explore students' ideas of whether they believe that people are born sporty, arty or intelligent. Teacher can ask the following questions: 'Was Michael Jordan born with a natural ability to slam dunk?' or 'Was Einstein born a genius?' Actually, Einstein did not talk until he was 4 and his teacher said that he was 'educationally subnormal'. Michael Jordan's coach said that he was not more gifted than the others; the only thing that differentiated him from his peers was the 'hard work and effort he put in'.

Teaching students about the brain and its amazing potential confronts the false assumption that the brain becomes 'fixed' at an early age. The evidence from neuroscience challenges this idea because it shows that our brain is making new connections every day. It continues to do this until the day we die. The more we use a new connection, the stronger that connection becomes, so the old saying that practice makes perfect is true! The brain rewires itself after damage (e.g., people learn to speak again after a stroke). It gets denser and bigger when we use it. One study looked at the brains of taxi drivers in London, and compared them to non-taxi drivers. The researchers looked at the area of the brain which deals with three-dimensional space: the hippocampus. What they found was that taxi drivers had a larger hippocampus than non-taxi drivers. A study of musicians found that the area of the brain that deals with processing sound, was bigger compared to that in non-musicians, and the area which controls fingers was also larger.

Some people believe that intelligence is carved in stone and unchangeable. This is called a *fixed* mindset. With this mindset, there is often a belief that intelligent people don't need to work hard at academic work and that failing at something is the result of a lack of intelligence, not lack of effort. With a *flexible* mindset, people see intelligence as malleable and changeable. For this group, learning takes a lot of hard work and effort. In this mindset, all individuals can learn and improve. Mindsets affect the goals people pursue, the effort they invest, and the way they deal with failure.

> Based on her empirical research, primarily with young people, Dweck (2006) concluded that people can be divided into two basic 'mindsets'. The first she calls the 'fixed mindset'. This mindset upholds the idea that people's ability is fairly fixed and not open to change. According to such a view, people are either intelligent, sporty, arty, good at maths, etc., or they aren't. This mindset also labels people according to personal characteristics. So people are good or bad, caring or selfish, and so on. It treats human capabilities and characteristics as if they were carved in stone and individuals as if they are finished products. In other words, it views human abilities and behaviours as innate, unchangeable things, like inanimate objects such as tables and chairs. The 'growth/flexible' mindset has a different starting point. It sees people as essentially malleable. In other words, they aren't fixed but have huge potential for growth and development.

Goals

Because people with a fixed mindset believe that potential and ability can be measured, they tend to create goals which are about demonstrating their ability (e.g., they believe that a grade A will show people that they are smart). People endorsing a flexible mindset tend to create learning goals. This is because they believe that intelligence is malleable and can be improved. Learning goals are about mastery (e.g., 'How well have I learnt this subject?'). People who set performance goals value looking good while people who set learning goals value learning.

> Dweck (2006) has shown that those who hold performance goals are less likely to work out of their comfort zone and try new and challenging things. This is because they might not do well – which would mean that they are not smart and this would reflect badly on them. Holding performance goals means that a student seeks to win positive, and avoid negative, judgements.

Failure

People adopting a fixed mindset tend to respond to failure with a 'helpless' response, while people with a growth mindset tend to respond to failure with a 'mastery' response. If a person believes that intelligence is fixed, something unchangeable, which you have a certain amount of and there is not much you can do to change that, then failure means that they are unintelligent. So they think there is no point in investing effort and as a result feel not motivated.

Effort

People with a fixed mindset avoid investing too much effort, because they believe that if they are good at something, they don't need effort to prove it. People with a flexible mindset, by way of contrast, value and invest effort because it brings mastery.

Class Activity 2: Possible or Impossible? (15 min.)
Small Group and Whole-Class Activity

Teacher splits the class into small groups of 5–6 students and gives them the Impossible/Possible handout with six statements. Students need to decide together whether these statements are true or false:

1. Finishing at the bottom of the class will never land you a good job.

2. You can't make art from decomposing rubbish.

3. You can't possibly fly abroad for less than £10.

4. Running a business from your bedroom is unlikely to get you far.

5. You can't be a world-class athlete without arms and legs.

6. Dreamers are losers.

When students report their conclusions back to the class, the teacher makes some comments on the chances of success by referring to some well-known personalities, companies and events:

1. Richard Branson has dyslexia and demonstrated had poor academic performance as a student. He never attended school after the age of 16.

2. French artist Fernandez Arman is world-famous for his 'accumulations' and destruction/ recomposition of objects, often at late stages of decay. For more information, see www. armanstudio.com.

3. Ryanair is a good example of the opposite.

4. This is exactly how Mark Zuckerberg created Facebook – from his Harvard dorm room.

5. Hilary Lister, the first female quadriplegic to sail solo around Britain September 2009.

6. As a motivation technique, Google uses a policy often called Innovation Time Off, where Google engineers are encouraged to spend 20 per cent of their work time on projects that interest them. Many of Google's newer services, such as Gmail, Google News, Orkut, and AdSense originated from these independent endeavours. This point can be supplemented by a short YouTube video obtained by searching for Googleplex.

Teacher summarizes the discussion by pointing out that most things are possible with some time and effort. Of course, the intention is not to argue that everything is possible, but rather to point out that the possibilities are far broader than what we expect.

> Ellen Langer's counter-clockwise study is a good foundation for the possibility argument. In this 1979 experiment, she and her students took elderly men away for a weekend retreat and asked them to live for a week as if it were 1959, when they were 20 years younger. As a result, these older men, many of whom could not even walk before, started walking and dancing, could hear and remember better, became happier and looked dramatically younger.

Next, the class works on three steps to develop a more flexible mindset.

Class Activity 3: Message from the Past (10 min.)
Individual Activity

Students are instructed to write a short note or a card to a person next to them about how abilities can be developed, with examples of how they themselves have dealt with some difficulties in the past or how they became good at something they were first bad at.

Class Activity 4: If Anything Was Possible (5 min.)
Paired Activity

Teacher asks students to tell a person next to them five things they would like to learn. They are encouraged to think broadly, as it can be anything, from dance, music, art to technology, sport or travel.

Summary and Homework (5 min.)
Teacher Instructions

Students are asked to identify someone they consider to be a hero. Using the internet and other resources, they need to find out the tremendous effort that went into their hero's accomplishments and write up to one page summarizing their story.

UNIT 4: POSITIVE MINDSET

Lesson 20: Hope

LESSON PLAN

Aims and Objectives	Resources
To be able to define hope To be able to distinguish the will from the way To understand the negative effects of unhopeful language	YouTube access I Hope handout My Hope Story handout Finding the Way handout Finding the Will handout

Class Activity 1: I Hope (5 min.)

Individual Activity/Working in Pairs

- Students complete ten sentences beginning with the words 'I hope . . .' on the I Hope handout.

- They exchange their notes in pairs, taking turns.

Teacher Explanation: The Importance of Hope (15 min.)

Teacher Lecture/Story/Group Discussion

- Benefits of hope, such as health and achievement, are discussed.

- Teacher reads a story to illustrate the role of hope in life-and-death situations and discusses the lessons from this story.

- Introduce the two components of hope, the way (or identification of multiple pathways to one's goal) and the will (agency, or motivation to keep going).

- Discuss some hopeful book and movie characters, identifying their goals, ways of achieving these goals and their willpower.

Class Activity 2: Finding the Way (10 min.)

Individual Activity

- Students select a goal they hope to achieve and complete the Finding the Way handout.

- They consider up to five different ways to reach this goal.

- They identify possible barriers to the goal achievement and find one more way to achieve their goal, despite the barriers.

Class Activity 3: Finding the Will (10 min.)

Individual Activity

- Students identify what can help them to keep going when things are tough and complete the Finding a Will handout.

- They also name personal characteristics that can help in this process.

Class Activity 4: Hope Talk (15 min.)

Whole-class Reframing Exercise

- Explain the negative effects of unhopeful language.

- Reframe ten unhopeful statements on the board together using Hope Talk.

- Illustrate with President Obama.

Summary and Homework (5 min.)

Teacher's Instructions

- Students need to write their personal hope stories in four paragraphs, using the four questions on the My Hope Story handout to guide them.

To download the student handouts and the PowerPoint slides for the lesson, please go to www.openup.co.uk/positivepsychology.

Lesson 20: Hope

HOW TO

Class Activity 1: I Hope (5 min.)
Individual Activity/Working in Pairs

Teacher asks students to complete ten sentences beginning with the words 'I hope . . .' on the I Hope handout.

They can then read their notes to another pupil, taking turns to listen.

Teacher Explanation: The Importance of Hope (15 min.)
Teacher Lecture/Story/Reflective Questioning

> Being hopeful is beneficial to one's psychological and physical health, for example, by buffering against interfering, self-critical thoughts and negative emotions. On top of this, hopeful people focus more on preventing ill-health, for example by taking more physical exercise. In addition, being hopeful substantially improves athletic and academic performance. This is thought to be because hopeful thinking allows people to create a mental plan that, when they focus on it, enables them to shut out interferences. Finally, being hopeful also increases the pain threshold for men (Curry et al. 1997; Snyder et al. 2005).

Hope is introduced as an emotion that reflects a positive expectation about something happening in the future. Being hopeful helps people to stay healthy, study better, win sports competitions and even cope with physical pain and troubles in life.

Whether someone is hopeful or not can have a significant effect in a life-or-death situation. Hope researchers tell the story of a patient who, when given an experimental drug for an incurable cancer, showed remarkable improvement until such time as the American Medical Association published evidence that the drug was ineffective as a cancer treatment. The patient, whose hope was now dwindling, died two days later (Snyder et al. 2002). Teacher can read the story of this case to students:

> Mr Wright had been diagnosed with cancer that had spread to various parts of his body. In the face of this untreatable disease, however, he had a strong desire to live. When he learned of a new drug called Krebiozen that was being given to persons with a more favourable prognosis than his, Mr. Wright asked his doctors to give him this experimental drug. After one injection, his condition improved. With continued treatments, most of the markers of his cancer had disappeared. Two months later, however, conflicting evidence about the effectiveness of Krebiozen was published. Concerned that Mr Wright's physical condition had returned to its previous grave status, his therapist decided to employ a placebo on the off-chance that improvement would occur again. The therapist told Mr Wright that

previous shipments of Krebiozen were made ineffective because of the way the drug was stored, and that it was, indeed, effective. Thereafter, Mr Wright was given the treatments from a 'new' batch of the drug (actually water), and he evidenced even more pronounced improvement in his cancer (as traced by objective indicators such as a radiograph) than had been the case the first time. For two months he was healthy and had no cancer symptoms. Then, the American Medical Association pronounced that Krebiozen was ineffective as a cancer treatment. Several days later, Mr Wright was readmitted to the hospital in a rapidly deteriorating state. His faith and hope, it was reported, were depleted. He died two days after entering the hospital.

Teacher reflect together with the class what they think might have gone on. Why is hope so essential to keeping going? Is there some hope in all situations? What is hope after all?

> According to psychologists, hope is actually both an emotion and the way we think. What this implies is that hope is not a fuzzy concept of wishful thinking, but is something quite tangible. The main researcher in this area, Rick Snyder, defines hope as an orientation towards the forming of goals. Hope is comprised of two components: (1) pathways (the way), or the perceived ability to generate many roads to one's desired goal; and (2) agency (the will), the perceived ability to sustain energy as one moves toward one's desired goal. Both components are necessary for hope to exist; neither is sufficient alone.

To introduce this concept to students, we feel hope if: (1) we know what we want and can think of several ways to get there; and (2) we start to act and keep on going. Pathway thinking (the way), or generating several workable routes to the goal, is very important because one route may not always be the best one. Even if the main route is blocked, a hopeful person will find other options open to them. However, knowing how to go about something is not enough, you need to get moving! This is where agency thoughts (or the will, represented as 'I can do this', 'I won't be stopped') come into play. These thoughts are not only about starting, but about staying energized and 'on task'.

Teacher asks students for some examples of characters who are hopeful (Chihiro in *Spirited Away*, Marlin in *Finding Nemo*). Can they identify the character's goal (e.g., to save parents), the way or ways in which they tried to do it (getting a job at the witch's house, travelling to the witch's sister, making friends with the baby) and the will or how they managed to do it (e.g., by keeping going because of the friendship with Haku, the River Spirit)? 'Just keep swimming, just keep swimming', sung by Dory in *Finding Nemo*, may be a good example of the will (available on YouTube).

Class Activity 2: Finding the Way (10 min.)
Individual Activity

Working with the Finding the Way handout, students need to identify one goal they hope to reach (they can use the results of the first activity to select from). This can be an object, or a certain thing they want to be able to do in school, or in sports. It could also be something to do with their family or friends.

The next stage is to identify up to five possible ways to reach this goal. Once completed, students need to think of what could go wrong, or possible barriers on the way to goal achievement. Finally, they need to find another possible way to achieve their goal that could help them navigate around these barriers.

> For those already hopeful, this exercise is likely to be straightforward, but for some students it may be difficult to identify more than one way to achieve a goal. It may be a good idea to ask those who complete this exercise quickly to help others.

Class Activity 3: Finding the Will (10 min.)
Individual Activity

If things get tough, or don't go according to plan, how can students find the energy to move toward their goals? Why would they keep going? What characteristics would help them to keep going? Students complete the Finding the Will handout, writing down the answers to these questions.

Class Activity 4: Hope Talk (15 min.)
Whole-class Reframing Exercise

Hope talk is a way of speaking that encourages hopeful behaviour. The teacher may want to convey to the students that the way in which they speak influences what they tell themselves and thus how they behave. If we constantly speak in unhopeful language to ourselves, we have less chance of moving toward our goals. Students are asked to rephrase the unhopeful statements on the board into ones filled with hope. Hope talk does not just mean 'thinking positively'. Instead, it has to do with a type of language that includes goal-oriented thinking and focuses on the opportunities side of a problem. It emphasizes pathways and ways around barriers as well. The teacher gives the first statement as an example and asks whether it sounds hopeful or not. How can students change it round into a more hopeful statement? How about 'Maybe I can learn to swim?' In what other ways can they improve it? Some further examples follow.

Unhopeful talk	Hope talk
I can't swim.	I don't know how to swim but I could try to learn.
I'm too nervous to talk in front of the whole school.	I think I should ask the teacher for some pointers on how to get rid of butterflies before my speech.
I'll never finish all my work.	I'll begin with this section and move on from there.
I missed five sets in the game this evening.	I'll practise tonight and we'll be better the next time round.
My friend hates me.	I've fallen out with my friend but we'll make it up tomorrow.
I hurt myself.	I hurt myself but it will heal soon.
I hate boring homework.	I'll do my boring homework and will look forward to watching a movie tonight.
My mum doesn't have any time for me.	My mum is very busy right now but I'll ask her to spend some time with me at the weekend.
I am not good at fixing things.	I'd better ask my dad to show me how to fix things.
I don't understand what the teacher is saying.	It's hard to understand what the teacher is saying but I am sure if I try hard enough, I can work it out.

Summary and Homework (5 min.)

Teacher's Instructions

The lesson can be concluded with a clip from YouTube, *Hope is Amazing and Inspiring* (it is better than the title suggests!). It can be found at: www.youtube.com/watch?v= BDU9OOw5pVM.

For homework, students need to write their personal hope stories in four paragraphs. They have four questions on the My Hope Story handout to guide them: What is my goal? What are the ways in which I can achieve it? What barriers am I likely to meet and how can I overcome them? What will help me to keep going?

UNIT 4: POSITIVE MINDSET

Lesson 21: Creative Problem-Solving

LESSON PLAN

Aims and Objectives	Resources
To learn and practise some problem-solving techniques	Superheroes handout Storyboard handout PowerPoint Lesson 21

Teacher Explanation: The Problem (5 min.)

Teacher Instructions

- As students come in, they see a PowerPoint slide saying 'Have you ever been dumped?' The next slide on the PowerPoint presents a dumping problem for discussion.

- Teacher asks students to form small groups of six and decide on the leader and timekeeper.

Class Activity 1: Solver-Songs (10 min.)

Teacher Instructions and Group Discussion

- Teacher explains that we can use some traditional methods to solve this problem (presenting examples), or we can try some less usual ones, based on associations.

- The first activity is to think of as many songs as possible that remind students of this problem (whole-class discussion). What solutions do these songs suggest?

Class Activity 2: Free Associations (10 min.)

Paired Activity

- Teacher explains the principle of free associations. Students carry out the exercise in pairs with the group leader overlooking the process.

Class Activity 3: Random Stimuli (10 min.)

Small Group Activity

- Teacher explains the principle behind random stimuli. All students first pick a random word and then a random object and relate it back to the problem.

Class Activity 4: Superheroes (10 min.)

Whole Group Activity

● After teacher's explanation, students choose a hero, write their 'super' characteristics and then use these to trigger some ideas.

Class Activity 5: Storyboards (10 min.)

Individual Activity

● Following an explanation, students engage with the storyboard technique.

Summary and Homework (5 min.)

Teacher Instructions

● Teacher discusses why these 'wacky' approaches to problem-solving are successful. For homework, students are asked to come up with their own 'messy' problem and practise one or more of these methods.

To download the student handouts and the PowerPoint slides for the lesson, please go to www.openup.co.uk/positivepsychology.

HOW TO

Teacher Explanation: The Problem (5 min.)

Teacher Instructions

As students come in, they see a PowerPoint slide saying 'Have you ever been dumped?' The next slide on the PowerPoint presents a dumping problem for discussion (it has been formulated for girls, but teacher may choose to adjust it for boys):

> Your boyfriend has just dumped you. You went out with him for three months and REALLY liked him. He sent you a text and said that he doesn't feel like going out with you anymore. You think your best friend might have something to do with it as you suspect they quite like each other.

Teacher asks students to form small groups of six and decide on the leader and timekeeper.

Class Activity 1: Solver-Songs (10 min.)

Teacher Instructions and Group Discussion

Teacher explains that we can use some traditional methods to solve this problem. These traditional methods usually require us to think really hard, for example, by brainstorming solutions or repeatedly asking 'why' to get to the heart of the problem. Alternatively we can try some less usual ones, based on associations and intuition.

> Considered the most complex of all intellectual functions, problem-solving has been defined as higher-order mental process that requires the modulation and control of more routine or fundamental skills. Problem-solving occurs when we needs to move from a given state to a desired goal state. Most traditional problem-solving techniques (e.g. brainstorming) are based on the analytic mode (Martin 2000). However, most of the techniques explored in this lesson are intuition based.

For the first activity, students are asked to think of as many songs as possible that remind them of this problem (whole-class discussion). It may be Gloria Gaynor's *I Will Survive*, Michael Jackson's *She's Out of My Life* or several of Lily Allen's songs, etc. Write these on the board and then ask the class what solutions these songs suggest.

Class Activity 2: Free Associations (10 min.)

Paired Activity

Teacher explains the principle of free associations. In this exercise, one starts with a given trigger and then 'travels' through the network of associations by simply saying or writing down the stream of ideas that come to mind, each idea triggering the rest until we reach one that seems promising. So, first of all, students need to think about the problem and notice the first word or sentence that comes to mind. Then they need to think about this word or sentence and say out loud anything else that first comes to mind, and so on. If something appears interesting, it's worth stopping and considering the value of this idea. For example, 'dumping' suggests 'a bin' that in turn suggests 'emptying' that further suggests 'empty mind'. How would one reach an empty mind? By meditation! So, one solution to the dumping problem may be to take up meditation and empty one's mind of thoughts and images associated with this relationship. Importantly, free associations can be really funny, wicked or bizarre (in the problem-solving literature a phrase 'throwing in a bunch of bananas' is often used to refer to these free associations).

> Free associations form the basis of most intuitive methods and rely on the mind's 'stream of consciousness'. Psychologist Guy Claxton (1998) distinguishes between the 'Hare Brain' (a speedy, analytical way of thinking) and the 'Tortoise Mind' (a slow, fuzzy, metaphorical, intuitive way of thinking). The Hare Brain actually suppresses innovation and creativity, while the Tortoise Mind encourages it. Techniques such as free associations are helpful for the latter.

Ground rules to take into account include *suspending judgement* (everything goes, whether or not it is rude, taboo, non-U, silly, unethical, politically incorrect, etc.), *being alert for 'bright' ideas* (everything that is particularly strong, intriguing, surprising, even if at first sight this does not appear to have direct relevance to the problem) and *expressing ideas in a 'do-able' format* ('blue' vs. 'I wish it was bluer').

Students apply the principle of free associations to the problem in pairs, with the small group leader overseeing the process and the timekeeper making sure their group is on time. Once finished, pairs should share their ideas and solutions with their small group.

Class Activity 3: Random Stimuli (10 min.)
Small Group Activity

Teacher explains the principle behind random stimuli. Students need to, once again, think about the same problem. Stimuli can be selected at random, by opening a book, looking out of the window, throwing a die, picking up any object, etc. This random stimulus can then be connected to the problem by either using it to find a solution or by creating a metaphor about this stimulus and then using this metaphor to find a solution. If one random stimulus does not work, it's worth picking another one and trying again.

> Many authors have suggested the use of random stimuli of various kinds (e.g., Henry 2001). These techniques (often called right-brain or whole-brain strategies) emphasize the basic importance of being open to possibilities from everywhere. In fact, random stimuli at first take our attention away from the task at hand, giving our Hare Brains a little rest. This time away is called *incubation* and is precisely an activity that helps our Tortoise Minds find a novel solution.

All students pick up a word at random (by opening a book, a notebook, a dictionary, etc. and placing a finger somewhere on the page with their eyes closed) and try to relate it back to the problem.

Next, they do the same with a random object that they either notice from the window or find in the classroom.

If the time permits, the teacher can explain the value of *incubation*. Incubation occurs when we keep the problem in mind ever so slightly (2 per cent) when we go for a walk or doing other activities throughout the day. If something draws our attention, we just need to note it down, because later this something may offer us a solution to our problem.

Class Activity 4: Superheroes (10 min.)

Small Group Activity

For this exercise, participants pretend to be a fictional (or real) superhero, ranging from the Incredible Hulk, Superman, James Bond and Catwoman to The Mask. Having selected a superhero, students write down this hero's characteristics (name, powers and weaknesses, history/background, costume details). Next, they get into the role and suggest solutions based on the hero, e.g. 'I am Superman and I can fly my friend who has betrayed me to the moon and leave him there, so that my ex-girlfriend would come back to me.' A milder version of this would be for the group to ask each of the group members in turn: 'How would such and such solve this problem?' Other members of the group can help too. Students who are introverted, shy or think the exercise is silly can use their non-imaginary heroes (celebrities, family members, scientists) to help them generate more novel solutions to the problem.

After the teacher's explanation, students choose a hero, write their 'super' characteristics on the Superheroes handout and then use these to trigger some ideas.

> This technique was created by Grossman and Catlin (1985, cited in Van Gundy 1988). Once again, it is intended to activate the Tortoise Brain (Claxton 1998).

Class Activity 5: Storyboards (10 min.)

Small Group Activity

Using the six boxes drawn on a piece of paper in the landscape position in the Storyboard handout, students need to draw the current problem in the first box and how they would feel if a good solution has been achieved in the last box. They then fill boxes 2–5 with the most important intermediate steps needed to reach a solution. At the end, some time can be spent looking at the sequence of pictures and thinking about what must be overcome in order to make this progression and achieve the desired goal. Following an explanation, students engage with the storyboard technique.

> Cartoon Storyboard technique was created by Henry (Henry and Mayle 2002). It is visual tool designed to develop a vision of a desired outcome and to identify the potential blocks that need to be overcome in order to achieve the goal.

Summary and Homework (5 min.)

Teacher Instructions

Teacher can conclude the lesson by discussing the following questions with the students:

● What is the difference between your usual homework (that often involves some traditional problem-solving) and what has been done during this lesson?

Solving school-assigned homework problems does not usually involve creative problem-solving because such problems are usually well defined and typically have well-known solutions. The problem tackled on this lesson is messy (or ill-defined; we don't really know why the break-up of this relationship occurred) and does not have only one solution, but, in fact, an unlimited number of solutions.

● This type of problem-solving requires creativity, but does creativity always require problem-solving?

Creativity does not always need a problem. We can use creativity to come up with a work of art, compose music and invent something that never existed before.

For homework, students are asked to come up with their own 'messy' problem and practise one or more of these methods to find a solution.

UNIT 4: POSITIVE MINDSET

Lesson 22: Money, Money, Money

LESSON PLAN

Aims and Objectives	Resources
To appreciate that having lots of money is not necessarily a good thing To appreciate the importance of goals–values concordance To discuss the idea of habituation	ABBA song Scenarios handouts x 6 (1 per each group)

Teacher Explanation and Class Activity 1 (15 min.)

Small Group Activity

- This lesson is completely activity-based.

- As students enter the classroom, teacher allocates them into groups of five and hands out their scenarios.

- The task of each group is to play-act a scene from the lives of their families, following conditions outlined.

- Each scene has to last no more than five minutes.

Class Activity 2: Scenes from Real Life (40 min.)

Role-play and Teacher-Led Discussion

- Groups play-act their scenes.

- If and when appropriate, the teacher comments on a scene or raises discussion questions to get the following points across:

  - Having enough money to satisfy our basic needs is important.

  - While having some money is important, more money is not necessarily better.

  - It is more important that your values and goals correspond well than simply having lots of money.

  - The pursuit of materialistic values can result in negative psychological consequences.

  - We get used to the amount of money we have very quickly.

Summary and Homework (5 min.)

Teacher Instructions

● Teacher invites the class to summarize the main points of the lesson.

To download the student handouts and the PowerPoint slides for the lesson, please go to www.openup.co.uk/positivepsychology.

Lesson 22: Money, Money, Money

HOW TO

Teacher Explanation and Class Activity 1 (15 min.)

Small Group Activity

> The importance of money is tricky to communicate and discuss, as anything other than 'lots of money is great' is quite likely to be rejected by this age group. The reason this lesson is completely activity-based is in order to allow relevant factors and doubts to be raised bottom-up rather than imposed from the outside. The teacher would need a lot of skill to notice appropriate moments and intervene with a comment or question when the right opportunity arises.

As students enter the classroom, teacher allocates them into groups of five and hands out their scenarios on the Scenario handouts (one per group). The first three sentences of each scenario are the same. They describe a family of four, with husband and wife aged 40 and 36, and children aged 14 and 8. The task of each group is to play-act a scene from the lives of their families, following conditions outlined. This scene has to have something to do with money and has to address both pros and cons of the situation. Each scene has to last *no more than five minutes.*

While most of the groups are likely to be able to create appropriate scenes, the teacher may have to offer a helping hand to one or more groups. Please find below some suggestions on the pros and cons of these families' financial situations.

> Habituation theory suggests that human happiness oscillates around a 'set point', thought to have a genetic basis. According to this theory, external circumstances and events will only influence happiness for a certain time period, after which it will gradually move back towards the set point. Habituation has been documented in lottery winners, who experience dramatic boosts in well-being on the dawn of their newfound economic status, only for the pleasure of the new lifestyle to fade over time (Brickman et al. 1978).

Scenario 1

Since winning the lottery two years ago, money is no object. The father quit his job as a teacher, mother as a nurse, and the whole family moved to Spain. Neither of parents works nowadays and they are occasionally bored. You live in a seven-bedroom villa with a large swimming pool, a pool bar and a tennis court. You employ a gardener, a cook, a maid and a chauffeur. Children are driven to their private school by a chauffeur. The family goes on holidays approximately six times a year.

- Pros: lots of money; freedom of action; rest; comfort; private schooling.
- Cons: boredom; loss of a meaningful activity; spoilt children; loss of old friends due to changing social class and moving countries; habituation; having to manage staff and a large house.

Scenario 2

You live in a yurt (a large weather-proofed Mongolian tent) all year round. Some people are calling you hippies. Both mum and dad make different bamboo structures (furniture and decorations) to bring in some small income. They enjoy their work because it's creative. Kids go to a local school; they have to walk for half-an-hour to get there. Sometimes you all go on an adventure holiday nearby.

- Pros: fresh air, creative job; low household expenses, close-knit family, adventurous holidays, exotic style of living.
- Cons: low-ish income; being perceived as 'weird'; not having many luxuries and comforts.

Scenario 3

Your family is predominantly self-sufficient. You live on a small farm and grow your own vegetables and raise pigs, cows, and chickens. Your house has solar panels and a small windmill in the garden. It doesn't provide you with all electricity that you need and goes off sometimes. Dad is an eco advisor for home owners. Mum does not work, but home-schools the kids. The family is strongly opposed to consumerism. You rarely go on holidays, as someone needs to look after livestock.

- Pros: natural living, high values–goals congruence (you do what you preach); contact with animals; organic food; not having to go to school.
- Cons: low-ish income; being perceived as 'weird'; not having many luxuries and comforts; not being able to leave the house to go on holidays.

Scenario 4

You are an immigrant family who has lived in London for the past 20 years. You own a small grocery store, so know the whole community really well. Both parents work in the shop. Kids also work in the shop after school and at weekends. You have a modest income, yet it is sufficient for your family needs and one summer holiday. The younger child goes to a local primary school, while the older one has to travel up to 40 minutes to his secondary school.

- Pros: OK income; shared family activity; kids earn their living; community spirit.
- Cons: kids have to work; secondary school far away; work may be repetitive; may be envious of other, better off families.

Scenario 5

You are what is often called a typical middle-class family. Dad is a busy accountant, who works at least six and occasionally seven days per week. Mum is a teaching assistant and only works school hours. You typically have two holidays per year – one in the sun and another skiing. Kids go to a local primary and a grammar school.

- Pros: good income; good standard of living; good holidays; good education.
- Cons: rarely seeing the father; life is too standard and predictable.

Scenario 6

You are a working-class family living in a house on a council estate. Mum and dad both lost their jobs in a supermarket earlier this year and have to rely on benefits to keep the family going. You have just enough money to get by, but would not be able to afford a holiday this year. Neither of the parents is particularly sorry about losing the job, as they did not enjoy them. They are both thinking about retraining. Kids go to a local school and mum and dad are both around to greet them on return.

● Pros: having a house inspite of not having a job, having an opportunity to retrain and do something that you love; having time; being at home for the kids.

● Cons: little money, no holidays, no employment.

Class Activity 2: Scenes from Real Life (40 min.)
Role-play and Teacher-Led Discussion

Groups play-act their scenes. Please ensure that no group takes more than five minutes to do so.

If and when appropriate, the teacher comments on a scene or raises discussion questions to get the following points across:

1. Having enough money to satisfy our basic needs (shelter, food, basic security) is important.

2. While having some money is important, more money is not necessarily better.

3. It is more important that your values and goals correspond well (you live what you preach), rather than simply having lots of money.

4. The pursuit of materialistic values can result not only in positive, but also in negative psychological consequences, like depression, anxiety and boredom.

5. We get used to the amount of money we have very quickly, usually within about three months.

It is more important that these points come across as natural and not premeditated than to mention all of them.

> Does money bring happiness? There appears to be a small overall correlation between income and well-being at any given point in time, which is even higher for people who have very little money. However, because of habituation, increases in income do not appear to equate to increases in well-being in the long term. Congruence between one's values and one's goals are a far more reliable predictor of well-being, as well as enjoying one's job and spending time with people we love. By and large, highly materialistic people are less happy, unless they fully achieve their materialistic objectives (Kasser and Ryan 1993; Biswas-Diener and Diener 2001).

Summary and Homework (5 min.)
Teacher Instructions

Teacher invites the class to summarize the main points of the lesson. There is no homework.

UNIT 4: POSITIVE MINDSET

Lesson 23: The Tyranny of Choice

LESSON PLAN

Aims and Objectives	Resources
To understand the 'costs' of excess choice To understand the difference between 'maximisers' and 'satisficers' To practise 'choosing when to choose'	Computers with internet access The Perfect Mobile handout Choosing When to Choose handout PowerPoint Lesson 23

Class Activity 1: The Task (5 min.)

Individual Activity

- As students come in, they find the Perfect Mobile handout on their desks.

- It provides a description of their 'identity' and asks them to choose the best mobile phone for that identity.

Class Activity 2: The Search is On (35 min.)

Paired/Small Group IT-based Activity

- In pairs or groups of up to three, students have half-an-hour to choose the best mobile phone for their character.

- The can use the internet and investigate any mobile networks possible.

- During the last five minutes of the task, they need to complete self-assessment questions underneath their identity description.

Teacher Explanation: The More, the Better? (10 min.)

Teacher-led Class Discussion and PowerPoint Presentation

- The final choice of each group is not the focus of attention.

- Teacher uses the experiences of students during the task and their reflections on the form to facilitate a discussion about the value of 'choice' in the modern society.

- Questions addressed could include feelings experienced during a difficult choice situation, difficulties in selecting the criteria, deciding when to stop and whether or not more choice is actually better.

- The teacher shows the slide highlighting the ridiculous amount of choice in our society, introduces the difference between maximizers and satisficers.

Summary and Homework (10 min.)

Teacher Instructions/Individual Activity

- If time permits, students complete the Choosing When to Choose handout.

- If not, this is their homework.

To download the student handouts and the PowerPoint slides for the lesson, please go to www.openup.co.uk/positivepsychology.

Lesson 23: The Tyranny of Choice

HOW TO

Class Activity 1: The Task (5 min.)
Individual Activity

As students come in, they find the Perfect Mobile handout on their desks. It provides a description of their 'identity' and asks them to choose the best mobile phone for that identity.

> You are a sales representative for a pharmaceutical company. You travel abroad approximately twice a month, mainly to Europe, but occasionally to Japan as well. Your phone is your lifeline and you use it every day. You typically receive 30–50 emails daily. When travelling, you are on your own a lot of the time. You are married, with two children whom you miss terribly when you are away. Your phone just packed up and you have a spare 30 min. before your next flight to buy another one. Your company would reimburse up to £100 of the phone value and would give you up to £20 per month. You really care about getting this phone right.

> In 2000 a professor of psychology at Swarthmore College, US, Barry Schwartz, published an article entitled 'Self-determination: the tyranny of freedom'. In it, he speaks of the psychological problems of freedom and autonomy, arguing that more choice is not necessarily good and, in fact, often makes our lives worse, rather than better.

Class Activity 2: The Search is On (35 min.)
Paired/Small Group IT-based Activity

In pairs or groups of up to three, students have half-an-hour to choose the best mobile phone for their character. They can use the internet and investigate any mobile networks possible.

> The point of this exercise is to create a sufficiently difficult situation of choice that students are able to realize that choice may have certain disadvantages, including difficulties in reaching a decision, information overload, error problems, as well as some psychological problems.

In the last five minutes of the task, they need to complete the self-assessment form underneath their identity description.

Teacher Explanation: The More, the Better? (10 min.)
Teacher-led Class Discussion and PowerPoint Presentation

The final choice of each group is not the focus of attention. Teacher uses the experiences of students during the task and their reflections on the form to facilitate a discussion about the value of 'choice' in the modern society. In addition to the questions on student handouts, teacher can discuss whether finding the perfect mobile phone is worth the effort and how students would feel if there were only about three phones to choose from.

It is important to lead this discussion in such a way that it achieves some wider generalizations. In the West, freedom, autonomy and choice are considered to be the conditions of psychological health. We believe that choice is good and more choice is better. Yet, research demonstrates that this is often not the case. Using the PowerPoint provided, the teacher shows the slide highlighting the ridiculous amount of choice we face on a daily basis and the 'costs' of making these choices:

● *Information problems* – how can we access all the information about the alternatives in order to make an informed choice?

● *Error problems* – with more complex options, we are more likely to make mistakes of judgement.

● *Psychological problems* – excess choice causes you to worry. It does not make you happier. In fact, quite the opposite – increased choice is accompanied by lower well-being. We also become demotivated to make a choice.

> There are several experiments showing that, instead of being liberating, choice can be demotivating. In one such experiment, participants were invited into a gourmet supermarket to taste a variety of jams. One group of people tasted six different types of jam, another 24, all of which were available for purchase. Some 30 per cent of people from the first group actually bought a jar, compared with just 3 per cent from the second group.

The teacher then introduces the two different types of 'choice' personality, highlighting the disadvantages associated with the second:

● *Satisficers* are people who just need to get what is 'good enough' for their requirements. They consider options until they find what meets minimum criteria, and then select that option.

● *Maximizers* are those who need to get absolutely the best deal and so look at all the possible options.

Summary and Homework (10 min.)
Teacher Instructions/Individual Activity

> Schwartz (2000) suggests that we can practise meta-choice and learn when choosing is worth it. In this way we can only be maximizers when it comes to something that really matters.

One solution to the problem of over-choice is deciding when choosing is worth it. If time permits, students complete the Choosing When to Choose handout. If not, this is their homework.

UNIT 4: POSITIVE MINDSET

Lesson 24: Think Yourself Happier

LESSON PLAN

Aims and Objectives	Resources
To understand which factors increase happiness To know what the happiness equation stands for To discuss the role of genes, circumstances and outlook	Happiness is Related to. . . Handout PowerPoint Lesson 24 Poster materials

Class Activity 1: I Would Be Happier if . . . (5 min.)
Individual Activity

● Students to complete the sentence 'I would be happier if . . .' out loud, as teacher notes their answers on a whiteboard.

Class Activity 2: Happiness is Related to . . . (5 min.)

Paired Activity

● Teacher gives us out the corresponding handout and asks students, in pairs, to decide whether these factors do or do not affect happiness.

Teacher Explanation: Understanding Happiness (20 min.)
Teacher-led Class Discussion and PowerPoint Presentation

● Using the PowerPoint presentation, teacher goes through each of the points in turn, offering further explanations when needed.

● Students are encouraged to articulate reasons for their own choices.

● Teacher writes the following equation on a whiteboard: H = SP+C+O and asks students what they think it stands for.

● Teacher explains the equation and defines Set Point, Circumstances and Outlook, asking the class to recall the factors that actively increase happiness.

Class Activity 3: The Poster (20 min.)

Small Group Activity

- In small groups students design a poster that reflects their learning about the equation.

Summary and Homework (10 min.)

Class Discussion

- Students summarize what they have learned today, show their posters to each other and celebrate one another's work.

To download the student handouts and the PowerPoint slides for the lesson, please go to www.openup.co.uk/positivepsychology.

HOW TO

Class Activity 1: I Would Be Happier if . . . (5 min.)
Individual Activity

Teacher asks students to complete the sentence 'I would be happier if . . .' out loud, and lists their answers on a whiteboard.

Class Activity 2: Happiness is Related to . . . (5 min.)
Paired Activity

Teacher gives out the corresponding handout entitled Happiness is Related to . . . and asks students, in pairs, to decide whether the factors mentioned do or do not affect happiness (are or are not important for happiness).

Teacher Explanation: Understanding Happiness (20 min.)
Teacher-led Class Discussion and PowerPoint Presentation

Using the PowerPoint presentation, teacher goes through each of the points in turn, offering further explanations when needed. At the same time, students are encouraged to articulate reasons for their own choices.

Optimism	increases happiness.
Feeling good about yourself (self-esteem)	increases.
Being nice	increases.
Living in a warm climate	makes no difference.
Old age	can increase happiness, contrary to popular belief.
Money	has a small positive effect but once basic needs are met the difference is negligible.
Gender	no difference (but girls show a greater range of emotions being both happier and sadder).
Close friendships	increase.
Marriage	increases (but only if it is a good marriage).
Work	increases (but unemployment decreases).

Children	both! (In the short term, research shows that having a family is hard work. However, research also shows that having children can make life more meaningful and people who are parents tend to live longer.)
Sleep	increases (but only if you are getting more than six hours a day and also not spending the day in bed!).
Religion	increases.
Meaning and purpose	increase.
Hobbies and activities	increase.
Watching TV	decreases.
Education	can increase, more so in the developing countries (but there is no link between IQ and happiness).
Being beautiful	no difference.
Winning the lottery	no difference (and can even make people less happy!).
Being famous	makes no difference.

> **Habituation, also called adaptation, is the process of people readily and rapidly adapting to positive circumstantial changes. Many studies have suggested this – a recent study of US students showed that the big and small events experienced by the students boosted or deflated their well-being, but only for a period of three months (Lyubomirsky 2007).**

Teacher writes the following equation on a whiteboard: H = SP+C+O and asks students what they think it stands for. Teacher explains that the H stands for Happiness and defines Set Point, Circumstances and Outlook.

$$Happiness = Set\,Point + Circumstances + Outlook$$

The set point is our genetic inheritance, which accounts for about 50 per cent of our personality. What that means is that roughly half our score on a happiness test is accounted for by the genes passed down to you by parents. This set point remains relatively stable through the lifespan and returns to its original point soon after most life events.

> **Psychologists used to believe that every emotional state and every personality trait could be improved. This was shattered in the 1980s when studies of identical twins – of which there have now been hundreds – showed that roughly 50 per cent of almost every personality trait turns out to be attributable to genetic inheritance (Seligman 2002).**

Our life circumstances can also change happiness for the better, but not by as much as we usually think – they account for about 10 per cent of your happiness. The reason they don't make us happier is because we get used to things very quickly and take them for granted. So although we find new things very exciting – such as pocket money, presents or new clothes – we very quickly *get used to them*.

Factors under outlook account for 40 per cent of the happiness make-up and these are the intentional things we can do to make us happier. Teacher asks the students what they think these factors could be. Ideas to include are:

- make lots of friends and be kind to them;
- be grateful for what you have on a daily basis;
- don't compare yourself to media stars or personalities;
- don't compare yourself badly with anyone;
- savour your life experiences.

But we have to work hard at these things. Lasting happiness lies within our reach, but we need to do something in order to achieve it.

So in summary, winning the lottery, being famous, getting rich or moving to a sunnier climate are not going to make us much happier! Being grateful, having friends, feeling good about yourself and being nice to others will!

Class Activity 3: The Poster (20 min.)
Small Group Activity

Teacher asks students, in small groups, to design an A4 poster that reflects what they have learned about the equation. Students are told that this poster is for other children aged between 10 and 13 and it should demonstrate, in a lively and understandable way, how to be happy.

Summary and Homework (10 min.)
Class Discussion

Students summarize what they have learned today, show their posters to each other and celebrate one another's work.

UNIT 5: POSITIVE DIRECTION

Lesson 25: Egg Yourself On

LESSON PLAN

Aims and Objectives	Resources
To understand the importance of motivation To learn and practise motivation strategies	I Have to – I'd Like to – I Want to handout Hard-Boiled Egg Strategy handout PowerPoint Lesson 25

Teacher Explanation (5 min.)

Teacher-led Class Discussion and PowerPoint Presentation

- Teacher starts the lesson with brainstorming around the question 'What have eggs got to do with motivation?'

Class Activity 1: Rotten Egg (5 min.)

Class Discussion

- 'Don't wanna do it, won't do it' is a 'rotten egg' solution. It applies when there is a strong dislike of, and no good reasons to engage in, a particular activity. Teacher asks the class for examples.

Class Activity 2: Fresh Egg (5 min.)

Individual Activity

- Fresh eggs are like intrinsic motivation. We do something because we really want to.

- Using the I Have to – I'd Like to – I Want to handout, students write as many things as they can under the 'I want to' heading.

Class Activity 3: Soft-Boiled Egg (15 min.)

Individual Activity

- Soft-boiled eggs are all about talking yourself into doing something.

- Using the I Have to – I'd Like to – I Want to handout, students write as many things as they can under the 'I have to' heading.

- Next, they need to re-write all their 'I have to's as 'I'd like to's, adding the reasons why.

139

Class Activity 4: Hard-Boiled Egg (5 min.)
Individual Activity

- Sometimes, a soft approach is not effective, we need to go a bit harder on ourselves.

- Students list everything that would go wrong if they don't act on their 'I have to's.

Class Activity 5: Scrambled Egg (5 min.)
Small Group Activity

- Turning something boring into something fun is the scrambled egg solution.

- Students brainstorm some strategies in their groups.

Class Activity 6: Creme Egg (5 min.)
Paired Activity

- Taking their most hated 'I have to', students consider rewarding themselves.

Summary and Homework (5 min.)
Teacher Instructions

- Students are asked to consider if there are any further 'motive-egg' solutions.

To download the student handouts and the PowerPoint slides for the lesson, please go to www.openup.co.uk/positivepsychology.

Lesson 25: Egg Yourself On

HOW TO

Teacher Explanation (5 min.)
Teacher-led Class Discussion and PowerPoint Presentation

At first sight, motivation may not appear as the most exciting of all subjects, yet it is incredibly important. Why do we get up in the morning? Why don't we just stay in bed all day, doing nothing? Motivation is the force behind getting up, going to work, opening a study book in the middle of the night, etc. Yet this force is not as simple as it looks on the surface and is not that easy to tame.

> Motivation is the activation or energizing of goal-oriented behaviours.

Teacher starts the lesson with brainstorming around the question 'What have eggs got to do with motivation?' This funky question, with no right or wrong answers, should hopefully start some thinking going.

After a few responses, teacher explains that the class will discuss a six-egg solution to all motivation problems. Despite appearing funny, all of these solutions are based on sound research.

Class Activity 1: Rotten Egg (5 min.)
Class Discussion

'Don't wanna do it, won't do it' is a 'rotten egg' solution. This solution represents what is called 'a-motivation' and applies when there is a strong dislike and no good reasons to engage in behaviour. Discuss whether this is a negative solution. It is not necessarily negative, because if we were motivated to do everything, we would simply not have enough hours in the day. Ask the class for examples (e.g. 'my parents want me to become a doctor, but I hate blood and all things biological').

Class Activity 2: Fresh Egg (5 min.)
Individual Activity

Fresh eggs represent intrinsic motivation. We do something because we really want to. Using the I Have to – I'd Like to – I Want to handout, students write as many things as they can under the 'I want to' heading. Entries may include eating, sleeping, chatting with friends, movies, computer games, etc. It is important to communicate the message that there are plenty of activities we want to do and that we don't need to do anything to motivate ourselves to engage with them, because the motivation is there already.

Intrinsic motivation reflects the inborn human tendency to seek out novelty and challenges, to explore the world, to exercise our capacities. When we are intrinsically motivated, we do something for the sake of it, simply out of enjoyment or interest. Intrinsic motivation is effortless, lasting and has many positive outcomes (Ryan and Deci 2000).

Class Activity 3: Soft-Boiled Egg (15 min.)

Individual Activity

Yes, there are plenty of activities we feel we have to do, yet don't particularly want to. All of these come under the heading of extrinsic motivation. All egg solutions from now on will address some aspects of extrinsic motivation. Soft-boiled eggs are all about talking yourself into doing something.

Using the I Have to – I'd Like to – I Want to handout, students first need to write as many things as they can under the 'I have to' heading. Next, they need to re-write all their 'I have to's as 'I'd like to's adding the reason for the change (because . . .). After the exercise, ask whether anyone feels more motivated to do any of their 'I have to' activities.

We are extrinsically motivated when we do an activity for the sake of something else or in order to attain some other outcome (e.g., going to work in order to earn money). However, extrinsic motivation is not all bad. It has to up to four different types, depending on how much our activities align with our likes, values and choices. All the exercises on this page utilize different strategies to make our extrinsic motivation more autonomous and therefore closer in function to intrinsic motivation. Autonomy is important because if we are relatively free to choose our actions or to be creative, then it's easier for us to appreciate the reasons for performing them.

Class Activity 4: Hard-Boiled Egg (5 min.)

Individual Activity

Sometimes, a soft approach may not be effective, we need to go a bit harder on ourselves. This is a boiled egg solution.

Using the Hard-Boiled Egg handout provided, students need to list everything that would go wrong if they didn't act on their 'I have to's. In a sense, they need to imagine the worst possible scenarios. These negative scenarios can be very powerful, but don't tend to exert an influence for long. In the short term, though (e.g., someone has a test tomorrow), hard-boiled eggs can be effective.

Class Activity 5: Scrambled Egg (5 min.)

Small Group Activity

Turning something boring into something fun is the scrambled egg solution. This solution requires creativity. One may think of combining their 'I have to's with existing 'I want to's, e.g. going running (I have to) with their friend (I want to hang out with her). Any out-of-the-box solutions are encouraged here.

Taking one of their 'I have to's as the starting point, students brainstorm some strategies in their groups.

Class Activity 6: Creme Egg (5 min.)
Paired Activity

Taking their most hated 'I have to', students could consider rewarding themselves for achieving something to which they aspire. It is important that they come up with the rewarding ideas themselves.

> Contrary to widespread practices, rewarding someone can actually undermine their motivation in the future. This is because we interpret rewards as someone attempting to control us. Self-rewarding is more straightforward, but should not be overused (Persaud 2005).

Summary and Homework (5 min.)
Teacher Instructions

Discuss which motivation solution was the most effective. At home, students are asked to consider if there are any further egg solutions.

UNIT 5: POSITIVE DIRECTION

Lesson 26: Nail, Nag, Nudge

LESSON PLAN

Aims and Objectives	Resources
To recognize the common experience of procrastination To learn some self-regulation strategies	YouTube video Nudge Competition handout

Teacher Explanation (5 min.)
Video Presentation and Class Discussion

● As students come in, they are shown a short procrastination video on YouTube.

● Teacher asks them whether they have ever put off doing an unpleasant task.

Teacher Explanation: 3Ns (20 min.)
Teacher Presentation and Class Discussion

● Teacher introduces the three main strategies for making a deliberate change: Nail (force oneself), Nag (convince/negotiate with oneself), and Nudge (create subtle reminders).

Class Activity 1: Me Today and Me Tomorrow (15 min.)
Role-play

● Students are asked to role-play the conversation between 'Me Today' and 'Me Tomorrow' using the suggested scenario.

Class Activity 2: Nudge Competition (15 min.)
Small Group Activity and Class Discussion

● In small groups of 5–6, students are requested to develop Nudge strategies for eating more fruit and vegetables on the Nudge Competition handout.

● The group with the highest number of workable strategies wins.

Summary and Homework (5 min.)

Teacher Instructions

● Students are asked to try all three deliberate self-discipline strategies during the following week and make a record of their results.

To download the student handouts and the PowerPoint slides for the lesson, please go to www.openup.co.uk/positivepsychology.

Lesson 26: Nail, Nag, Nudge

HOW TO

Teacher Explanation (5 min.)

Class Discussion

As the students come in, they watch a short procrastination video on YouTube, that can also be found using 'Tales of mere existence: Procrastination' search words:

http://www.youtube.com/watch?v=4P785j15Tzk.

Teacher asks them whether they have ever put off an unpleasant task. Searching for examples, the teacher initiates the discussion about what happened next. Did the situation become worse after a while?

> Procrastination refers to the deferment of actions or tasks to a later time. Psychologists often see such behaviour as a mechanism for coping with the anxiety associated with starting and/or completing any task or decisions. For a behaviour to be classified as procrastination, it must be counterproductive, needless and delaying (Sapadin 1997).

Teacher Explanation: 3Ns (20 min.)

Teacher Presentation and Class Discussion

> Self-discipline is the ability to get yourself to take action regardless of your emotional state. It is about being able to accomplish a certain task or to adopt a particular pattern of behavior, even if one would rather be doing something else.

So how do we make ourselves do something, rather than putting it off? Teacher introduces the three main strategies for self-discipline/self-regulation: Nail (force oneself), Nag (convince/negotiate with oneself), and Nudge (create subtle reminders).

● The first strategy, *Nail*, is what we often spontaneously resolve to do when trying to achieve self-discipline, for example, giving up smoking, losing weight or starting to do homework at the same time every day. We force ourselves. Unfortunately, this is usually unsustainable because after a short while we rebel, and lapse into the old pattern of behaviour. The Nail strategy is what many (unsuccessful) New Year resolutions are based on.

> In self-determination theory terms, the Nail strategy is akin to introjected regulation — when we initiate the change out of guilt towards ourselves. Unfortunately, guilt is not a lasting motivator.

● The second strategy, *Nag*, is about convincing ourselves. In order to do so, we need to give ourselves good reasons to make a change and acknowledge that we actually have a choice (we can decide to do it one way or another, or not at all). We need to sympathize with the way we feel (e.g., it is important to recognize that the change may not be the most pleasant experience to begin with, yet it may still be worthwhile). Importantly, successful changes are often based on having a good support network, i.e., friends who help us in the change-making process.

> By way of contrast, the Nag strategy is based on identified regulation. We make changes because we find that they are personally meaningful and valuable for us, and thus we feel more autonomous and committed to them (Ryan and Deci 2000).

● According to a dictionary, to nudge is 'to push against gently, especially in order to gain attention or give a signal'. *Nudge* as a theory of self-discipline is not very different. Nudge relates to anything that influences our choices. Using research, it demonstrates that our decisions and behaviours are influenced by how the choices are presented. For example (this is quite funny!), sketching a small black fly in a urinal – first tried in men's restrooms at Amsterdam's Schiphol Airport – turns out to be amazingly effective at getting men to pee straight, reducing spillage by 80 per cent. Why? Because men have a deep-seated instinct to aim at targets . . .

A school cafeteria might try to nudge kids toward good diets by putting the healthiest foods at front, while putting less healthy junk food in harder to reach places. Students thus are not prevented from eating whatever they want, but the arranging of the food choices in that way has the effect of decreasing consumption of junk food and increasing consumption of healthier foods.

Many institutions, including governments, can make life easier for people by gently nudging them in directions that will make their lives better. This can be achieved by better investments for everyone, more savings for retirement, less obesity, more charitable giving, and an improved educational system. However, it takes some thinking to find these clever ways of presenting choices to promote positive change.

> We often think that human beings are smart and always clear about their own interest. Trouble is, we aren't like that: we eat too much and drink too much (sometimes at the same time) and we don't hit the gym or save enough. Nudge suggests ways in which we can do the right thing, by advocating a default choice that helps individuals make a 'better decision' about their lives. Behavioural research shows that people taking financial decisions are frequently inclined to reach incorrect conclusions because of limited or poor quality information. Many people might know (or suspect) they are not saving enough for their retirement, but few have a real grasp of how much they should be saving to avert poverty in their old age. And even for those who do struggle with willpower, saving can always be done later; the temptation to spend is stronger in the here and now. So, for example, making a pension plan a default, rather than optional, choice (Thaler and Sustein 2008).

Class Activity 1: Me Today and Me Tomorrow (15 min.)

Role-play

Students are asked to role-play the conversation between 'Me Today' and 'Me Tomorrow' using the suggested scenario below. This exercise is about getting cross with oneself for not starting some job earlier, and ending up with a lot to do at the last moment or jeopardizing some arrangements. Me Today could argue the point of taking time off today and postponing things for tomorrow. Me Tomorrow can argue from the perspective of the implications of having to do the job today that should have been done yesterday, and therefore not being able to get some deserved rest.

Scenario: You have a week left to complete a four-week project. You have not even started. It is a very important project and you have a chance to do it well, but need to devote all the time you have left to it.

To carry out this activity, teacher picks some students who are usually good in coming up with ideas on the spot and asks them to perform in front of the class.

Class Activity 2: Nudge Competition (15 min.)

Small Group Activity

Teacher presents the problem of children and teenagers not eating their necessary 'five-a-day' every day. In small groups of 5–6, students are requested to develop Nudge strategies for eating more fruit and vegetables and complete the Nudge Competition handout. The group with the highest number of workable strategies wins.

Summary and Homework (10 min.)

Teacher Instructions

Teacher asks the class to recall the three strategies covered during the lesson. Students are asked to try all three deliberate self-discipline strategies during the following week.

UNIT 5: POSITIVE DIRECTION

Lesson 27: The Flow Zone

LESSON PLAN

Aims and Objectives	Resources
To understand what flow is and the main principles governing flow To identify students' flow-inducing activities	YouTube access Gaffa tape Paperclips PowerPoint Lesson 27

Teacher Explanation (10 min.)
Visualization/Class Discussion

- Teacher runs the 'Flow Zone' visualization and asks students what activity they were visualizing.

- The concept of 'Flow' was conceptualized by Mihaly Csikszentmihalyi. Teacher shows a funny YouTube clip to see others struggle with his name!

Teacher Explanation: What is Flow? (15 min.)
Teacher Presentation and Class Discussion

- Teacher draws out the flow diagram (with gaffer tape) on the floor of the classroom.

- Students are introduced to the 'diagram' and discuss the sections of Flow, Anxiety and Boredom.

Class Activity 1: Your Activity Zones (15 min.)
Group and Individual Activity

- Students walk around the diagram and as they stand in each section, they identify the activities that might lead them to feel in that zone.

Class Activity 2: The Paperclip Exercise (10 min.)
Small Group Activity and Class Discussion

- The Paperclip Exercise is introduced as a means to increase the 'flow zone'. In 5 minutes, each small group is to identify as many uses for a paperclip as possible.

Summary and Homework (10 min.)

Teacher Instructions

- Students to commit to carrying out one flow activity.

- They are also to choose one boring activity and decide how to make it more challenging.

To download the student handouts and the PowerPoint slides for the lesson, please go to www.openup.co.uk/positivepsychology.

Lesson 27: The Flow Zone

HOW TO

Teacher Explanation (10 min.)
Visualization/Class Discussion

> The concept of 'Flow' is important for students as strong feelings of being in flow are vital for motivation, positive emotion, higher levels of concentration, a greater sense of control and satisfaction (Parr 1998).

The teacher asks students to close their eyes and asks them to 'imagine a moment in time when you are doing something that is totally absorbing to you. You are lost in this activity and completely involved in it. It's challenging yet energizing. It's fascinating and you know that you can do it. You're surprised how time flies, as you're so in to what you are doing.'

The students are then asked to give the teacher ideas of the activities they were imagining and are explained that this state of mind is called 'Flow' which has been defined as being 'a state of mental operation in which the person is fully immersed in what he or she is doing, coupled with a feeling of energized focus, full involvement and success in the process of the activity'. This concept was developed by a psychologist called Mihalyi Csikszentmihalyi (cheeks-sent-me-high). The teacher then plays the YouTube clip of young children trying to pronounce this name (it's funny):

www.youtube.com/watch?v=TjXqdAYUG48.

Teacher Explanation: What is Flow? (15 min.)
Teacher Presentation and Class Discussion

> The concept of flow came to Csikszentmihalyi in the 1960s when he was researching the creative process. During his interviews with dedicated artists he was struck by how they would often ignore hunger, discomfort and fatigue while working on a painting, yet lose interest in the work as soon as they were finished. When observing rock climbers and musicians he found much the same thing.

Teacher explains to the students that the key to creating flow is to establish a balance between skills and challenges: 'Whether you are playing football, doing your homework, going shopping or playing with a Nintendo, if the challenges of the situation overwhelm your level of skill, you will feel anxious or frustrated. On the other hand, if the activity is not challenging enough, you will become bored.'

153

This is shown visually by laying out a matrix on the floor with gaffer tape (this can be shown on PowerPoint too, but allowing the students to walk around will heighten their learning).

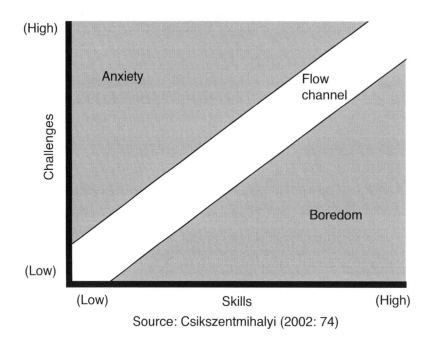

Source: Csikszentmihalyi (2002: 74)

In 2003, a longitudinal sample of 526 high school students across the US investigated how adolescents spent their time in high school and the conditions under which they reported being engaged (Shernoff et al. 2003). Unsurprisingly, students experienced increased engagement when the perceived challenge of the task and their own skills were high and in balance – a necessary condition of flow. What is perhaps surprising is their articulation of the need to have the learning environment under their control, with instruction relevant to their lives. Results of the study showed that students spent approximately one-third of their time passively attending to information transmitted to the entire class, with only 14 per cent dedicated to interactive activities.

These findings are echoed in two studies with Italian adolescents analysed in 1986 and 2000 (Bassi and Della Fave 2004). Again, the school setting did not seem to provide the appropriate environment for enjoying learning, with 'class work primarily associated with apathy' (2004, p. 172). Instead, the experience of flow was provided by structured leisure activities; studying at home; video game playing and interactions with their peer group.

The Flow Channel

The Flow Channel is where the challenge equals one's skills to meet it.

Anxiety Sector

A big challenge but little skill (examples: not revising for an exam; being asked to take on a new challenge which everyone else knows how to do).

Boredom Sector

No challenge and you know how to do it (examples: watching TV; subjects one finds too easy).

The teacher demonstrates the matrix with an example such as learning tennis: 'at the beginning you don't have much skill but the challenge is low (holding your racquet correctly) – therefore you are in the flow zone. As you start to learn tennis, if your teacher is still showing you how to hold the racquet you will experience boredom. Therefore, as we master a new skill, the challenge has to increase in order to stay in flow!'

Class Activity 1: Your Activity Zones (15 min.)
Group and Individual Activity

The students are asked to walk around the matrix and, as they stand in each section, to identify the activities that might lead them to feel in that zone. Students are to draw out the diagram in their Well-Being Diaries and record the activities they have identified in each section.

> One study followed talented teenagers over a four-year time span. Those who, at age 13, had identified their talent area as a source of flow and who experienced relatively more flow and less anxiety during school activities, were more likely to stay committed to their talent through the teen years (as opposed to disengaging from it). There is a book dedicated to flow and teenagers called *Talented Teenagers* (Cskiszentmihalyi et al. 1993).

Class Activity 2: The Paperclip Exercise (10 min.)
Small Group Activity and Class Discussion

Teacher explains that one beneficial aim in life is to increase our 'flow zone', or the time we spend in this state. There are several reasons for doing so:

- Flow activities are fun and enjoyable.

- The enjoyment we get from flow is generally lasting and reinforcing.

- We want to repeat the activity as we get a natural 'high' from it.

- To continually experience flow, we are constantly striving, growing, learning and generally increasing our happiness and overall well-being.

We can do this in two easy ways: (1) do more flow activities; and (2) turn boring activities into challenging activities.

> The concept of being 'in the zone' may have originated from Gallwey (1975) who documented the benefits of flow in the famous sports psychology book, *The Inner Game of Tennis*. The benefits of flow are also well researched and documented by Csikszentmihalyi (2002); and Lyubomirsky (2007).

Now the paperclip is introduced. The teacher asks the class to form small groups. Each team is given a handful of paperclips. In five minutes, each small group is to identify as many uses of a single paperclip as possible. This is a competitive exercise and the group with the most uses wins!

Summary and Homework (10 min.)

Teacher Instructions

Students are asked to recap what they have learned about flow and are asked to commit to choosing one flow activity that they could increase and spend more time doing. Also the teacher asks students to choose one boring activity and decide how to make it more challenging and record outcomes in their Well-Being Diaries.

UNIT 5: POSITIVE DIRECTION

Lesson 28: Big Hairy Goals

LESSON PLAN

Aims and Objectives	Resources
To understand why goals are important To use the Wheel of Life and choose goals to pursue To understand how to set a stretch goal To understand the importance of taking action	The Circle of Life handout Buddy 'PREP-are' handout Footprint handout PowerPoint Lesson 28

Class Activity 1: The Circle of Life (10 min.)

Individual Activity

As students enter the classroom, teacher hands out the Circle of Life handout, reads the instructions and asks the students to fill it in.

Teacher Explanation (10 min.)

Teacher PowerPoint Presentation

- Teacher explains the importance of setting goals and shows success statistics of goal setters.

- Next, teacher explains the difference between slack, stretch and scary goals and show students the four factors of a stretch goal (Personal, Realistic, End point, Positive = PREP).

- The students are asked to look at their Circle of Life handout and choose one goal they want to work on.

Class Activity 2: PREP-are Yourself! (10 min.)

Paired Activity

- The students are asked to find a 'buddy' and help strengthen one another's chosen goal using the flowchart provided (incorporating the PREP questions) on the Buddy 'PREP-are' handout.

Class Activity 3: Big Hairy Goals (25 min.)

Teacher Explanation/Small Group Activity

- Teacher introduces the concept of Big Hairy Goals and asks each individual to choose their own BHG, which can be as unusual as they like. So how do we take action on goals?

- Teacher asks the class to form into groups of approximately six people and hand out five A4 Footprint handouts to each group, which should be laid out in front of each team (Action Alley).

- Teacher then explains the exercise and demonstrates with personal BHG.

Summary and Homework (5 min.)

Small Group Activity

- Students are reminded of the three main learning points of the lesson.

To download the student handouts and the PowerPoint slides for the lesson, please go to www.openup.co.uk/positivepsychology.

Lesson 28: Big Hairy Goals

HOW TO

Class Activity 1: The Circle of Life (10 min.)
Individual Activity

As students enter the classroom, the teacher hands out the Circle of Life handout. The students are asked to read the handout and start filling it in.

> The Circle of Life is a familiar goal-setting technique for helping people decide areas of their life that they want to work on. This Circle of Life has been specifically designed for adolescents and contains six factors: Family; Friendships; Fun; Financial; Flow; and Fitness.

The students need to consider each of the areas and mark each area out of 10 for satisfaction. 1 is very dissatisfied and 10 is very satisfied. There are some questions on the handout to help guide the students.

> Fortunately, there is abundant goal-setting research, probably because scientists recognize that, to a great extent, our well-being depends on our ability to choose a direction in life and follow preferred pathways (Schmuck and Sheldon 2001).

Teacher Explanation (10 min.)
Teacher PowerPoint presentation

The basics of goal research are outlined on the PowerPoint presentation. Having goals is considered by many scholars as the basis of all human behaviour – it's that important! If an individual is making progress towards a goal, he/she is happy; if failing or facing setbacks, he/she is frustrated and angry. These scientists suggest that every action humans take is as a result of this fact.

> Two scientists are prominent in the belief that the pursuit of goals is the basis of all human behaviour directing our emotions, positively or negatively, depending on our progress of attainment (Carver and Scheier 2002).

What the science has shown (as detailed on the PowerPoint slides) is that effective goal setting increases performance by up to 19 per cent and predicts success in later life. However, the type of goal that is set is important. Goals can be characterized into three areas:

● Slack goals – goals that are really easy to achieve and, in effect, could be done in one's sleep. They are unchallenging but achievable.

- Stretch goals – goals that are achievable but challenging.

- Scary goals – goals that are so big, they are just plain scary!

Students should be aiming towards setting Stretch goals. There are four factors that can be considered essential elements of a good Stretch Goal:

1. **Personal** – a personal goal belongs to you. You have chosen it and are motivated to achieve it. It isn't a 'should-do' goal that someone else has told you to do.

2. **Realistic** – when a goal is unrealistic, it becomes a scary goal and we are much less likely to take action to achieve it.

3. **End point** – all goals need to be time-bound with some idea as to when they will start and end and what the conclusion will look like. Without this, a goal will drift on forever.

4. **Positive** – a good goal will be stated in the positive, which is towards rather than away from.

> **Results from a review of laboratory and field studies on the effects of goal setting on performance show that in 90 per cent of the studies, specific and challenging goals led to higher performance than easy goals (Locke et al. 1981).**

At the end of the PowerPoint presentation, the students are asked to look at their Circle of Life and choose one goal they would like to work on.

Class Activity 2: PREP-are Yourself! (10 min.)

 Paired Activity

The students are asked by the teacher to find someone they want to work with. They are distributed the flow chart handout, headed 'Buddy PREP-are'. The teacher explains to students that they are going to help each other clarify and strengthen their chosen goal using the flow chart provided. Each pair has five minutes to interview their buddy and work their way down the flow chart to success!

> The flowchart contains PREP questions with 'yes' and 'no' directions and hints as to how to strengthen each stage of the goal-setting process.

> **Scientists have also shown that well-being is enhanced when goals are feasible, realistic, personally meaningful and directed at a 'towards' motivation (Lyubomirsky 2001).**

Class Activity 3: Big Hairy Goals (25 min.)

Teacher Explanation/Small Group Activity

The teacher explains to the students that what really counts in achieving goals is breaking the goal down into small steps and taking action. Once action is taken, the impetus propels the goal forward. Teacher explains that in many big businesses people choose what are called Big Hairy Audacious Goals (pronounced Bee-HAGS) to motivate people to take action. The students are going to do something similar.

Ask each individual to choose a Big Hairy Goal for themselves – the madder the better! Give some examples:

- End world poverty.

- Live in Australia.

- Solve climate-change problems.

- Win *The X Factor*.

- Become a famous footballer.

> 'Big Hairy Audacious Goals' is a phrase coined by Collins and Porras in 1996 and further developed in their business articles and books for *Harvard Business Review*.

The teacher lays out five footprints in a line on the floor and calls it Action Alley. The students are told that they are going to tell the group their BHG, and then walk through five steps they could take that would form a realistic starting point to achieving their BHG.

For example, to live in Australia, you could:

Step 1: Ask around and find someone who either lives there or has lived there.

Step 2: Find out the pros and cons of living there.

Step 3: Go online and check out the immigration rules.

Step 4: Find out what qualifications you would need.

Step 5: Find out what careers they accept.

> Researchers are interested in why so many people fail to achieve their goals. The lack of taking action (or giving up the action you started) is one of the main reasons goals are either not started, or stopped after a short period of time (Ford and Nichols 1991).

For each step, the teacher takes one step up the Action Alley on one footprint, taking a maximum of five steps. Afterward the students are asked to do the same.

Summary and Homework (5 min.)

Class Discussion

The students are reminded of the three main learning points of the lesson. These are:

1. Goal setting is really important in life and directs behaviour and emotions.

2. Set 'stretch' goals that are challenging but not too scary.

3. Above all, take action!

UNIT 5: POSITIVE DIRECTION

Lesson 29: Five Little Pigs

LESSON PLAN

Aims and Objectives	Resources
To define time perspective To identify their own preferred time perspective To understand the differences between time perspective types	PCs with internet access PowerPoint Lesson 29

Teacher Explanation (5 min.)

Teacher Presentation

- Teacher introduces the notion of time perspective (TP) to students. Our time perspective is the kind of glasses we habitually put on when we look at the world around us. These glasses represent the way we deal with time and affect many actions we take.

Class Activity 1: What Glasses Do You Wear? (30 min.)

Individual Activity

- Using computers, students complete the Zimbardo Time Perspective Inventory.

- Students record their results in their class workbooks, identifying whether or not each TP type is prominent for them.

Teacher Explanation: Five Little Pigs against the Wolf of Time (20 min.)

Teacher PowerPoint Presentation and Class Discussion

- There are five main sub-types of time perspective: future, past-negative, past-positive, present-hedonistic and present-fatalistic.

- Using the pictures of pigs on the PowerPoint to illustrate the concepts, teacher introduces TP profiles to students.

- Students are asked to raise hands if they have scored above 50 per cent on the profile under discussion.

Summary and Homework (5 min.)

Teacher Instructions

● Students are asked to remember their top time perspective and observe for a week how their actions match their time perspective's description.

To download the student handouts and the PowerPoint slides for the lesson, please go to www.openup.co.uk/positivepsychology.

HOW TO

Teacher Explanation (5 min.)

Teacher Presentation

The teacher introduces the notion of time perspective to students. Our time perspective is the glasses we habitually put on when we look at the world around us. These glasses represent the way we deal with time and affect many actions we take. They have three main types of lenses: past, present and future. Some of us are here-and-now people. Some of us are stuck in the past. Some of us, when choosing between work and play, usually go for work while others select play.

> Scientifically, time perspective (TP) has been defined as a preferential direction of an individual's thoughts towards the past, present or future, which exerts a dynamic influence on their experience, motivation, thinking and several aspects of behaviour. Lennings highlights both cognitive and affective aspects of the construct in his definition of TP as 'A cognitive operation that implies both an emotional reaction to imagined time zones (such as future, present or past) and a preference for locating action in some temporal zone' (1996, p. 72).

Class Activity 1: What Glasses Do You Wear? (30 min.)

Individual Activity

In order to find out about their own time perspective, the teacher asks the students to take the Zimbardo Time Perspective Inventory: available at:

www.thetimeparadox.com/surveys/ztpi/.

The students are asked to record the results in their class workbooks. They are explained that, to understand their results, students need to compare them with the following graph (also on PowerPoint). To help them, their workbooks will ask them for each TP type and whether or not in their case it's higher or lower than in 50 per cent and 84 per cent of people.

The bold dots on the graph represent the ideal time perspective.

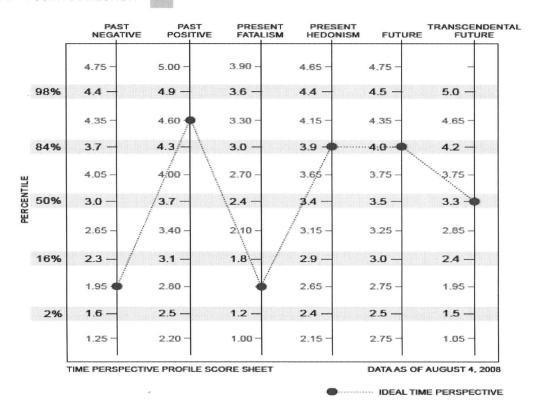

	PAST NEGATIVE	PAST POSITIVE	PRESENT FATALISM	PRESENT HEDONISM	FUTURE	TRANSCENDENTAL FUTURE
	4.75	5.00	3.90	4.65	4.75	–
98%	4.4	4.9	3.6	4.4	4.5	5.0
	4.35	4.60	3.30	4.15	4.35	4.65
84%	3.7	4.3	3.0	3.9	4.0	4.2
	4.05	4.00	2.70	3.65	3.75	3.75
50%	3.0	3.7	2.4	3.4	3.5	3.3
	2.65	3.40	2.10	3.15	3.25	2.85
16%	2.3	3.1	1.8	2.9	3.0	2.4
	1.95	2.80		2.65	2.75	1.95
2%	1.6	2.5	1.2	2.4	2.5	1.5
	1.25	2.20	1.00	2.15	2.75	1.05

PERCENTILE

TIME PERSPECTIVE PROFILE SCORE SHEET   DATA AS OF AUGUST 4, 2008

●·········· IDEAL TIME PERSPECTIVE

If they are below 50 per cent, they can treat this TP as low (or very low if below 16 per cent). If they are above 50 per cent, they can treat this TP as high (or very high if above 84 per cent).

Teacher Explanation: Five Little Pigs against the Wolf of Time (20 min.)

 Teacher PowerPoint Presentation and Class Discussion

There are five main sub-types of time perspective: future, past-negative, past-positive, present-hedonistic and present-fatalistic. Now that the students know their score on each, it is important to introduce them in more depth. Use the pictures of pigs on the PowerPoint to illustrate the concepts (you may also want to name the pigs).

> Although TP may be affected by situational forces, such as going on holidays or being under stress, it can become a relatively stable personality characteristic. So usually, people tend to have one dominant temporal perspective.

The person who is predominantly *Future-oriented* is concerned with working for future goals and rewards, often at the expense of present enjoyment, delaying gratification and avoiding time-wasting temptations. People with future TP are more likely to floss their teeth, eat healthy foods, revise well and get medical check-ups on time. They also tend to be more successful than others. The third little pig, who built his house from bricks, adequately estimating the dangers from the wolf, was surely a future-oriented pig.

> TP is a powerful influence on many aspects of our behaviour, including education, achievement, health, sleep, romantic partner choices, and more.

The *Present-hedonistic* person lives in the moment, is a pleasure seeker, enjoys high-intensity activities, seeks thrills and new sensations and loves adventures. Children are primarily present-hedonistically oriented. Unfortunately, such behaviour can have negative consequences. Present-hedonists are at risk of giving in to temptations leading to virtually all addictions (e.g., alcohol and drug abuse), risky driving, accidents and injuries, and academic and career failure. The *Present-fatalistic* person, contrariwise, is helpless, hopeless and believes that outside forces control their life.

The past TP is all about focusing on family, tradition, continuity of self over time, and a focus on history. This can be either positive or negative. The *Past-positive* person has a warm, pleasurable, often sentimental and nostalgic view of their past, and values maintaining relationships with family and friends. He/she loves stories about the good old times. The *Past-negative* person feels haunted by the past, focusing on personal experiences that were aversive or unpleasant.

> Not only people, but also even nations and cultures, can have their own time perspective biases. Protestant and individualistic nations tend to be more future-oriented than Catholic and more collectivistic ones. The former are usually better off financially than the latter. In the northern hemisphere, people living in southern areas are more present-oriented than those in the north (possibly because they like to spend time enjoying the sunshine).

As the teacher introduces each TP profile in turn, they ask for a show of hands (non-obligatory, they may choose to only do it for positive TPs).

Summary and Homework (5 min.)
Teacher Instructions

Students are asked to remember their top time perspective and observe for a week how their actions and behaviour match this time perspective's description.

UNIT 5: POSITIVE DIRECTION

Lesson 30: The Balancing Act

LESSON PLAN

Aims and Objectives	Resources
To understand the advantages and disadvantages of each TP profile To learn about the importance of a balanced time perspective	PowerPoint Lesson 29 YouTube video

Teacher Explanation (5 min.)

Teacher Presentation and Class Discussion

This lesson builds on the previous one.

- Showing the pictures of the pigs only, the teacher asks students to define each TP profile.

Class Activity 1: Who Is Happy? (10 min.)

Class Discussion

- Students try to guess which one of these time perspective pigs is likely to be happier.

- Teacher communicates the scientific results, highlighting the advantages and disadvantages of each TP profile.

Teacher Explanation: The Balancing Act (5 min.)

Teacher Presentation

- Teacher explains that each of the TP types may have some personal value, but if it becomes excessive and excludes or minimizes the others, then it may become dysfunctional.

- Teacher introduces the balanced TP.

Class Activity 2: Time Strategies (35 min.)

Small Group Activity and Video Presentation

- Three broad groups are established to work on the increase of one of the constructive TP profiles: past-positive, present and future (in order to become more balanced overall).

- Each of the groups brainstorms strategies (with teacher's help).

- Groups present their suggestions back to the class.

- Teacher shows the YouTube video *A Jar of Life*.

Summary and Homework (5 min.)
Teacher Instructions

- Students are asked to think what the rocks, gravel (pebbles) and sand in their lives are.

To download the student handouts and the PowerPoint slides for the lesson, please go to www.openup.co.uk/positivepsychology.

HOW TO

Teacher Explanation (5 min.)
Teacher Presentation and Class Discussion

Showing the pictures of the pigs only, the teacher asks students to define each TP profile. Teacher encourages the typical representatives of each profile to reflect on their behaviour and attitudes.

Class Activity 1: Who Is Happy? (10 min.)
Class Discussion

The students are asked to guess which one of these time perspective pigs is likely to be happiest. The past-negative and present-fatalistic pigs are pretty unhappy. They don't think there is anything they can do to feel better. The future pig is actually neither happy nor unhappy because he is too busy studying and thinking about the future. He is, however, very productive and proud of his achievements. The present-hedonistic pig feels quite good when he is engaged in pleasurable activities, but is not very happy with his life because of feeling guilty for not studying and working enough.

> A large number of researchers claim that a focus on the future is fundamental to well-being and positive functioning. Yet the drawbacks of excessive future orientation include workaholism, neglect of friends and family, not taking time for occasional self-indulgence, and not having time for hobbies. Many other scholars think that a time orientation with a focus on the present is a prerequisite for well-being. However, this orientation has downsides as well, including the neglect of long-term consequences and 'the morning after' feelings.

The time perspective that is the best for well-being is the past-positive orientation. Past-positive-oriented individuals have the highest self-esteem and are satisfied with their past and present life. However, even this very positive perspective has its own drawbacks, which include being excessively cautious, avoiding change, sustaining the status quo, even when it is not in one's best interest, and trying to apply old solutions to new problems. So, is developing the past-positive TP the best one could do?

Teacher Explanation: The Balancing Act (5 min.)
Teacher Presentation

The teacher explains to students that each of the TP types may have some personal value, but if one becomes excessive and excludes or minimizes the others, then it may become dysfunctional. There are costs and sacrifices associated with emphasizing any individual TP, whether the focus is on achievement-oriented, 'workaholic' future TP, on hedonistic present, or on nostalgic past (which is an infrequent TP in modern society). Here is where the ideal of a *balanced* time perspective

171

comes into play. It is a more positive alternative to being a slave to any particular temporal bias. A balanced TP means scoring above average on the 'positive' TPs (past-positive, present-hedonistic and future) and low on the two 'negative' TP types.

What does it mean to have a balanced TP? People with a balanced time perspective are capable of adopting a temporal perspective appropriate to the situation they find themselves in. So when they spend time with their families and friends, they are fully with them, connecting and enjoying each other. When they take a day off work, they can rest rather than feel restless. However, when working and studying, they approach a situation from the perspective of the future and work more productively. A capacity to focus, flexibility and 'switch-ability' are essential components of a balanced TP. Although a balanced TP is hard to achieve, it seems to offer a key to the work–life balance and a sense of well-being. People with a balanced TP are much happier overall.

Class Activity 2: Time Strategies (35 min.)
Small Group Activity and Video Presentation

The teacher establishes three broad groups to work on the increase of one of the constructive TP profiles: past-positive, present and future (in order to become more balanced overall). The students are asked to allocate themselves into these groups on the basis of their preferred area for self-development.

> Teacher may choose to add some groups working on strategies for decreasing certain TP profiles, either the negative or excessive positive ones.

The students are then asked to brainstorm the strategies of how to increase their group's time perspective. They will need to present the strategies back to the group, so could put the outcomes of their work on the flipchart.

While students are engaged with this exercise, teacher can circulate around the class and help them with some ideas:

● Past-positive – making memories, visiting family members, presents, getting in touch with friends from primary school, looking through a photo album.

● Present-hedonistic – listening to music, doing something fun/hobbies, taking time off.

● Future – making long-term and short-term plans, diary, to-do lists.

As the groups present their strategies back to the class, teacher explains that in trying to make one's life more balanced, we need to address the important things first. The YouTube video *A Jar of Life* illustrates this point well:

www.youtube.com/watch?v=Lpau5YXk46Yandfeature=related.

> This is a very good illustration of priorities, so if the teacher is feeling brave, they may want to do it themselves rather than showing the video. They would need a jar, rocks, pebbles and sand as materials.

Summary and Homework (5 min.)
Teacher Instructions

Students are asked to consider what the rocks, gravel (pebbles) and sand in their lives are.

UNIT 6: POSITIVE RELATIONSHIPS

Lesson 31: Tonic or Toxic?

LESSON PLAN

Aims and Objectives	Resources
To understand the basis of a healthy friendship To recognize the elements of good and toxic friendships To learn to use the DESC model to handle tricky situations	The Conflict Questionnaire handout The Managing Tricky Situations handout PowerPoint Lesson 31

Teacher Explanation: Healthy Friendships (5 min.)

Teacher Discussion

- The importance of friendships is introduced from social, scientific and evolutionary perspectives.

Class Activity 1: Tonic Versus Toxic (10 min.)

Paired Activity and Class Discussion

- Students are to list out all the characteristics of a great friendship and all the characteristics of a toxic friendship.

- Teacher collects their ideas on the whiteboard.

Class Activity 2: Rocky Responses (10 min.)

Individual Activity/PowerPoint Presentations

- A friendship is easy to sustain when times are good, but has to be worked at when it hits difficult times.

- Students complete the conflict questionnaire and call out their preferred responses to each of the situations.

Teacher Explanation: Managing Your Responses (15 min.)

PowerPoint Presentation

- The four different responses to tricky situations are introduced, together with the consequences of each response.

- Students learn the four-point model for handling crucial conversations using the DESC model.

Class Activity 3: The Bumpy Road (15 min.)

Small Group Activity

- Students form small groups of approximately five people and create two difficult friendship scenarios.

- They practise the first three stages of the DESC model and feedback on their experience.

Summary and Homework (5 min.)

Teacher Instructions

- The lesson is summarized by explaining how important good friendships are in life and how students' ability to manage friendships through difficult times will prove to be an important skill in developing their self-confidence.

To download the student handouts and the PowerPoint slides for the lesson, please go to www.openup.co.uk/positivepsychology.

Lesson 31: Tonic or Toxic?

HOW TO

Teacher Explanation: Healthy Friendships (5 min.)

Teacher Discussion

> In recent decades, the centrality of confident personal relationships to happiness has been amply borne out by scientific research. Adolescents who have good relationships with their peers are found to be happier, on average, than those whose peer relationships are less than satisfactory. Equally, students with good relationships also tend to be more successful at school and later on in life, at work and financially (summarized in Martin 2006).

The ability to make, maintain and – sometimes – to break friendships is a mark of the confident person. Adolescents who lack confidence often maintain friendships that are unhealthy and eventually damage their self-esteem, whereas confident students will make and maintain healthy, long-lasting friendships that increase each person's self-esteem.

From a scientific point of view, being connected with good friends is essential for happiness, health and success. From an evolutionary point of view our species is designed to live in relatively small social groups, surrounded by individuals who are familiar to us and with whom we conduct complex and subtle relationships. Given that the students live in a social networking age, collecting vast numbers of virtual friends, it is vital to stress that it is the *quality* of friendships that counts in developing long-lasting and positive friendships, not the *quantity*.

> Two evolutionary biologists, Charles Darwin and, more recently, Robin Dunbar (2005) spearheaded our knowledge of social relationships and their importance in today's society.

Class Activity 1: Tonic Versus Toxic (10 min.)

Paired Activity and Class Discussion

Students are requested, in pairs, to list all the characteristics of a great friendship and all the characteristics of a toxic friendship and collect their ideas on the whiteboard.

For a good friendship, the answers could include:

● trust

● having fun together

● laughter

- looking for the good in one another

- sharing experiences and having shared experiences

- asking one another for help

- being there for one another when times are difficult

- similar values/being like one another

- forgiveness and making up.

> Trust is the single biggest factor that will dictate a positive friendship. Once trust is destroyed, it is hard for a friendship to get back on track (Keller and Wood 1989).

For a toxic friendship, the answers could include:

- betrayal of trust

- jealousy

- bitching behind one's back

- seeking out the negative

- turning your back when times are difficult

- lack of forgiveness.

Class Activity 2: Rocky Responses (10 min.)

Individual Activity/PowerPoint Presentations

A friendship is easy to sustain when times are good, but the measure of a good friendship is what you do when the friendship is tested.

The first thing for the students to consider is how they respond to potential conflict. To help them, students complete the Conflict Questionnaire handout. The questionnaire contains four questions and the students have to choose one of four responses. The four responses are as follows:

a) = aggressive responses
b) = assertive responses
c) = passive responses
d) = manipulative responses.

> The questionnaire builds on the well-documented work of scientists Thomas and Kilmann. They devised the questionnaire as a research tool in 1974 and it has been widely used in schools and organizations. Their work led them to conclude that adults and children respond alike to tricky situations through accommodation, aggression, collaboration or withdrawal.

Teacher Explanation: Managing your Responses (15 min.)

Teacher PowerPoint Presentation

Using the PowerPoint presentation, teacher first of all reads out the brief situation, asking the students for all the potential reactions to this situation. Responses are grouped into the four specific behaviours for the students. The presentation discusses the 'why's and 'consequences' of the four different behavioural responses of passivity, aggression, manipulation and assertion.

Next, students learn the four-point model for handling crucial conversations using the DESC model. *DESC* stands for *Describe, Express, Specify,* and *Consequences*:

1. *Describe.* Describe the behaviour/situation as completely and objectively as possible. Just the facts! 'When I said that I wanted to take up running, you laughed at me.'

2. *Express.* Express your feelings and thoughts about the situation/behaviour. Try to phrase your statements using 'I', and not 'You'. Beginning sentences with 'You' often puts people on the defensive, which means they won't listen to you. 'As a result, I felt demotivated and that you were teasing me.'

3. *Specify.* Specify what behaviour/outcome you would prefer to happen. 'I don't enjoy being teased and I would prefer you to just support me.'

4. *Consequences.* Specify the consequences (both positive and negative). 'If you help me, I'll have more energy and I won't be sitting in front of the TV all the time!'

Here is a quick, practical summary of the model:

- When you. . . (do whatever they have done)
- It makes me think and feel . . .
- What I would prefer is . . .

DESC has a fourth stage, 'Consequences', but it is important that students practise the first three stages well first, otherwise the consequence stage can sound threatening or aggressive.

> The DESC script was developed by Bower and Bower (1991). The DESC script has been used extensively in organizations with adults and children for the past 15 years and is a simple and effective method of developing assertion.

Using one of the scenarios from the questionnaire, students run through an example using DESC, for example:

> When you talk about me behind my back it makes me think that we are not such good friends after all, which makes me unhappy. What I would prefer is for you to tell me something is wrong before you tell others and then we can sort it out together.

A second example from the questionnaire could be:

> When you are always late to meet me, it makes me feel stupid hanging around for you. I would really like it if you could turn up on time in the future.

Class Activity 3: The Bumpy Road (15 min.)

Small Group Activity

To really understand the first three stages of DESC, students are asked to form small groups of approximately five people. They need to create two difficult friendship scenarios and then to take turns practising the three stages of DESC, using the handout.

Students feedback their experience to the teacher and, if time allows, discuss when they will feel comfortable being this assertive and when they might find it trickier to use.

Summary and Homework (5 min.)

Teacher Instructions

Healthy friendships are an essential ingredient for a happy life but, like a garden, they take work and effort in order to maintain in a healthy state. Ignoring problems is not the hallmark of a good friendship, but assertive conversations are.

UNIT 6: POSITIVE RELATIONSHIPS

Lesson 32: Forgiveness

LESSON PLAN

Aims and Objectives	Resources
To understand the importance of forgiveness To practise letting go of grudges To write a forgiveness letter	Forgiveness Letter handout

Teacher Explanation (10 min.)
Class Discussion/Reflective Questioning

- Teacher discusses with students quotes on forgiveness, continuing with a more general discussion on forgiveness and letting go of grudges.

- The concept of forgiving being an act of courage is introduced.

Class Activity 1: How I Felt (10 min.)
Paired Activity

- In pairs, students share two situations each:

  - a time when they were angry with someone (friend or family member);

  - a time when they were forgiven by someone.

Teacher Explanation: Learning to Forgive (10 min.)
Group Discussion

- The first step in forgiveness is recognizing how we feel when we are forgiven by someone else.

- Teacher offers background knowledge to forgiveness and the three parts to forgiveness.

- Class discusses why we find it hard to forgive, yet harbouring resentment hurts mostly ourselves.

Class Activity 2: The Forgiveness Letter (20 min.)

Individual Activity/Group Discussion

- Students' task is to write a Forgiveness Letter. This letter is private and does not need to be sent to someone.

- Students offer some reflections on how it felt to write the forgiveness letter.

Class Activity 3: Wishing Others Well (5 min.)

Visualization

- Students carry out a brief visualization exercise, encouraging them to value forgiveness.

Summary and Homework (5 min.)

Teacher's Instructions

- Students take their forgiveness letter home to re-read it in private. They are to reflect on whether they would like to send it to the intended recipient, or re-write and send it.

To download the student handouts and the PowerPoint slides for the lesson, please go to www.openup.co.uk/positivepsychology.

Lesson 32: Forgiveness

HOW TO

Teacher Explanation (10 min.)
Teacher-led Class Discussion/Reflective Questioning

Forgiveness is an important strength for building good relationships and is closely related to empathy, the ability to understand the feelings of others. As one of the VIA Signature Strengths, forgiveness plays a central part in positive psychology and is especially important to adolescents. This is the time when peer relationships are widespread: both perceived and real insults are common and often resentment and anger interfere with fulfilling friendships. This means there are ample opportunities within school life to build students' capacity to forgive and let go of grudges.

Teacher discusses with students the following quotes on forgiveness, continuing with a more general discussion on forgiveness and letting go of grudges.

> There is no love without forgiveness and there is no forgiveness without love. (Bryant McGill)
> To forgive is to set a prisoner free and discover that the prisoner was you. (Lewis Smede)
> The weak can never forgive. Forgiveness is the attribute of the strong. (Mahatma Gandhi)
> The stupid neither forgive nor forget. The naïve forgive and forget. The wise forgive but do not forget. (Thomas Szasz).
> Forgiveness is the oil of relationships. (Josh McDowell)

Finally, the concept of forgiving being an *act of courage* is introduced. Students are asked to consider what this may mean.

> Seligman (2002) discusses the value of forgiveness in acknowledging that someone did you wrong but removes the 'sting' and can even transform the experience. Seligman describes empirically validated studies that document the positive effect of forgiveness, including less anger, more optimism, and better health. Additionally, research has found that forgiveness correlates with overall life satisfaction in a sample of college students (Peterson and Seligman, 2003).

Class Activity 1: How I Felt (10 min.)
Paired Activity

In pairs, students are instructed to discuss two instances involving forgiveness (per person). The first instance is when they have felt angry towards someone. Guiding questions might include:

● How did you feel in this situation?

● In what ways did it feel good to hold a grudge?

● In what ways did it feel bad to hold a grudge?

● What happened to the relationship/friendship as a result?

● If the grudge ended, how did that happen?

The second incident needs to be related to when they have been forgiven by someone else. Guiding questions could be:

● Who forgave you?

● How did this feel?

● What happened to the relationship/friendship as a result?

> Research indicates that we are more likely to be able to forgive when we remember first how we have been forgiven and how this felt (McCullough 2001).

Teacher Explanation: Learning to Forgive (10 min.)
Group Discussion

Teacher questions how students felt about being forgiven and explains that the first step in being good at forgiveness is to remember how good it feels to be forgiven by someone else. They explain that grudges interfere with our ability to feel close to other people and to have fun together and that the ability to forgive is a strong predictor of leading a happy life: 'You can let go of grudges by thinking about what you like most about the person and what life would be like without this person in it, but it is up to you to decide whether or not it makes sense to forgive.'

> Research studies by Seligman have demonstrated that negative thinking and catastrophizing make small transgressions seem much bigger than they actually are (Seligman 2002). This work is further explained by Fox Eades in her (2008) book, *Celebrating Strengths: Building Strengths-based Schools*.

Forgiveness involves three elements:

● Our feelings towards somebody who has hurt us.

● Our thoughts about the person who has hurt us.

● Our behaviour towards a person who has hurt us.

It feels hard to forgive because someone has hurt our feelings or behaved wrongly towards us. This means we can start a cycle of revenge, avoidance, of anger, disappointment or hostility. This can further initiate a negative downward spiral that can have a lasting impact for children, particularly at school. Therefore we have to make a *conscious* effort to feel more positively towards someone who has acted in such a way. Tolerance and the ability to see another's point of view are important aspects for children to learn.

Psychologists who study forgiveness define it as a shift in thinking, such that your desire to harm that person has decreased and your desire to do them good has increased. It is not seen as reconciliation, nor a pardon, or condoning or excusing the behaviour. 'Forgive and Forget' is also a misnomer as you do not have to forget – merely contemplate the injury from arm's length. (Lyubomirsky 2007)

Class Activity 2: The Forgiveness Letter (20 min.)
Individual Activity/Group Discussion

Students' task is to write a forgiveness letter to a person who might have upset their feelings, said something hurtful or behaved meanly towards them, using the Forgiveness Letter handout. This might be a friend or a family member. They are provided with the following instructions:

- Explain what was done to you in detail.

- Show how you were affected by it at the time (what you thought; how you felt).

- State what you wish the other person had done instead.

- End the letter with a statement of forgiveness and understanding (for example, 'I realize now that what you did was the best you could do at the time and I forgive you').

Students discuss how it felt to write the forgiveness letter (which they may have found hard). If it was too hard, students can put the letter aside and try again in a few days or weeks. Teacher explains forgiveness is a skill and needs to be practised and they have just taken a very important first step.

The Forgiveness Letter is a validated exercise within Positive Psychology designed by Lyubomirsky (2007).

Class Activity 3: Wishing Others Well (5 min.)
Visualization

Students carry out a brief visualization exercise, encouraging them to value forgiveness. They are asked to close their eyes and picture themselves giving a good gift to someone they like, saying something kind and imagine how this feels for both parties. Now they are asked to imagine giving another gift to someone they don't like, and again saying something kind to this person. After they imagine if they could do this to all the unkind people they come across, they have the control and capability to spread good feelings. This will send the important message that they can choose to work on their feelings towards others (Fox Eades 2008).

Summary and Homework (5 min.)
Teacher's Instructions

Students take their forgiveness letter home to re-read it in private. They are to reflect on whether they would like to send it to the intended recipient, or re-write and send it. However, they can equally choose to do nothing with this letter – it is a personal choice. The purpose of the homework is to encourage purposeful reflection on this subject.

UNIT 6: POSITIVE RELATIONSHIPS

Lesson 33: Listening and Empathy

LESSON PLAN

Aims and Objectives

To learn the principles of empathic listening

To understand how to respond actively and constructively

To practise seeing a situation from another point of view

Resources

Internet access and projector
Whiteboard and marker

Teacher Explanation (5 min.)

Teacher-led Class Discussion/Reflective Questioning

- Teacher introduces the concepts of listening and empathy.

- Students are asked to define 'empathy' and confirm the importance of listening.

Class Activity 1: 'Can You Hear Me?' (15 min.)

Paired Activity/Group Discussion

- Teacher sets up A and B Listening Exercises as per teacher guide.

- Students are asked how they felt when they were ignored and when they were listened to.

Teacher Explanation: Active Constructive Responding (15 min.)

Teacher-led Discussion

- Teacher explains to students the principles of empathic listening and introduces them to the concept of 'Active Constructive Responding'.

- Teacher to demonstrate with an example each of the four ways one can respond.

Class Activity 2: 'Respond to Me, Please!' (15 min.)

Paired Activity/Group Discussion

● Teacher asks the students to find a different person to work with than in the last exercise. Set up Active Constructive exercise as per teacher guide.

Summary and Homework (10 min.)

Group Discussion

● Teacher discusses with students how they found responding actively and constructively.

● What did they notice and what will they do in the future?

● Students to choose three people with whom they would like to practise active constructive responding. These could be friends, family members or teachers.

To download the student handouts and the PowerPoint slides for the lesson, please go to www.openup.co.uk/positivepsychology.

Lesson 33: Listening and Empathy

HOW TO

Teacher Explanation (5 min.)

Teacher-led Discussion/Reflective Questioning

Building social resources, in this case, the ability to empathize and truly listen to someone else is central to positive psychology. The ability to listen and understand someone else builds positive emotions which in turn starts a positive upward spiral of tolerance, creativity and well-being. When we are happy, we are less self-focused, we like others more and we want to share our good fortune, even with strangers. When we are down, we become distrustful, turn inward and focus on ourselves.

> In the past, psychologists assumed that unhappy people – identifying with the suffering they know so well – would be more empathic and altruistic. In the last decade, experiments have shown that happy children and adults display more empathy and are willing to donate more money to others in need (Seligman 2002).

Students are asked to define 'empathy'. Some scientific definitions include:

- a sense of shared experience including physical and emotional feelings;

- understanding another person's feelings by imagining or remembering being in a similar position yourself;

- putting yourself in someone else's place and imagining how that person must feel.

Teacher explains that in order to have empathy with someone and understand how they feel, we first of all have to listen – properly!

Class Activity 1: 'Can You Hear me?' (15 min.)

Paired Activity/Group Discussion

The class is asked to form pairs, in each pair there is A and B.

Round 1

- A is instructed to talk to B for one minute about a topic that excites them (this could be a holiday; a hobby; an adventure).

- B is instructed to deliberately not listen. They should not speak and should appear uninterested and distracted. They should not leave their seat, however (i.e., they cannot walk away).

- The teacher starts Round 1 and stops the exercise as soon as 60 seconds is up.

Round 2

● A is instructed to continue talking for a further minute (again about a topic that excites them).

● B is instructed to deliberately listen this time. They should act genuinely interested (without going completely over the top!).

● The teacher starts Round 2 and stops the exercise as soon as 60 seconds is up.

Students are asked to tell the teacher the emotional effect it had on them when they were being ignored, and when they were being listened to, and teacher confirms with students how important it is for us to be listened to.

> This exercise originates from an excellent book called *Listening* by Ian Mackay (1984). Variations of this exercise are run in SEAL and counselling training.

Teacher Explanation: Active Constructive Responding (15 min.)
Teacher-led Discussion

> Researchers have established that not only is listening the key to success with regards to understanding and empathizing but also helps children learn more effectively. Research conducted by Dr Steil demonstrated that of the four key skills for children – listening, speaking, reading and writing – listening was the most used skill (45 per cent) but the least 'taught' skill. Speaking was the next most used skill (30 per cent) but the next least taught skill. Writing was the least used skill (9 per cent) but the most taught skill (Mackay 1984).

Based on their exercise, the students are asked to summarize how we usually demonstrate positive and negative listening and list these ideas on the whiteboard. Some ideas are as follows.

Positive listening:

● sympathetic gestures;

● proximity;

● smiling;

● eye contact;

● lots of non-verbal agreements (nodding, etc.).

Negative listening:

● distance;

● no eye contact;

● no smiling;

● turned away;

- downcast eyes;

- fidgeting.

> The background to the research on Active Constructive Responding (ACR) is when psychologists discovered that what distinguishes good and poor relationships is not how the partners or friends respond to one another's disappointments or bad news, but how they respond to good news. This compelling work was conducted by Shelly Gable and Harry Reis, as they asked the question, 'What do you do when things go right?' (Gable et al. 2004).

Students are introduced to the concept of Active Constructive Responding. Shelly Gable, Assistant Professor of Psychology at the University of California, has examined the different types of response we give to other people's good news. She explains that we can respond in four different ways.

Teacher draws the following on the whiteboard, while demonstrating the four ways of responding through an example of 'telling a friend you have just won a sports prize'.

Active and Constructive
'That's great! Wow! I know how hard you worked for that. Let's go and tell Annie and Theo as they'll be really pleased for you too!'
(Lots of eye contact; displays of positive emotion; smiling; touching; laughing.)

Passive and Constructive
'Oh right. Well done.'
(Little or no active emotional expression. Not really listening.)

Active and Destructive
'I'm surprised. There were lots of other really good people going for that prize. You'll probably have to do more at sports day now.'
(Displays of negative emotion; no smiling.)

Passive and Destructive
'I'm off to my next lesson.'
(Ignoring; no eye contact; no acknowledgement; turning away or leaving room.)

> One study demonstrated that people who tried to respond actively and constructively three times a day over the course of just one week became noticeably happier and less depressed (Schueller 2006).

Class Activity 2: 'Respond to Me, Please!' (15 min.)

Paired Activity/Group Discussion

Students are asked to find a different person to work with than during the last exercise. Again, have an A and a B person. Ask A to choose a piece of good news and tell B this piece of good news. They are going to tell this piece of news to B four times, and each time, B is going to respond in a different way according to the chart above.

They must swap over when they have gone through all four responses.

Important note: When giving an active and constructive response you do not need to overdo the praise and positive feedback. This can make people feel uncomfortable. Instead concentrate on asking questions that encourage the person to talk about their good news and thereby you both get to savour the positive emotion. When responding actively and constructively, encourage the students to ask at least three questions.

Summary and Homework (10 min.)
Group Discussion

Teacher discusses with students their responses to this exercise. For instance:

● How easy did they find it to respond actively and constructively?

● How often do we do this?

● How often do we find ourselves reacting in a passive way because we're not really listening?

● What causes us not to listen to others?

● What might cause us to respond in a destructive way?

Teacher explains that Active Constructive Responding is a learned skill to build relationships with others by focusing on their good news.

Students are to choose three people with whom they would like to practise Active Constructive Responding. These could be friends, family members or teachers.

UNIT 6: POSITIVE RELATIONSHIPS

Lesson 34: Sweet Trading

LESSON PLAN

Aims and Objectives	Resources
To understand the principles of negotiation To be able to apply these principles to everyday life	Sweet Trading handout 60 sweets (10 of each type) PowerPoint Lesson 34

Teacher Explanation (10 min.)

Teacher Explanation

● Teacher introduces the purpose of the lesson and why negotiation is such an important life skill.

● Students are told that they are going to be playing an experiential game called Sweet Trading that combines planning and trading to understand the basics of negotiation.

Teacher Explanation (10 min.)

Teacher Discussion and PowerPoint Presentation

● Teacher divides the students into ten teams, each of three people, and hand out their written brief, which contains the scoring and rules. Do not hand out sweets at this stage.

● The brief is read out aloud with the students to ensure they understand what they are going to have to do.

● Teacher runs through the basics of planning on the attached PowerPoint presentation.

Class Activity 1: Planning Sweet Trading (10 min.)

Small Group Activity

● Teacher hands out the sweets (ideally in a brown paper bag) to each team. A random selection of six sweets should be given to each team.

● Each team is given 10 minutes to make a plan. No trading should happen in this time.

Class Activity 2: Let the Trading Commence! (20 min.)
Small Group Activity

● Students are allowed to trade for 15 minutes.

Summary (10 min.)
Teacher-Led/Whole Class Discussion

● Teacher collects in the final points from each team.

● Teacher explores what went well, what did not go so well and what the students learned about negotiation.

● Teacher reiterates that the skill of negotiation is one of life's broadest and most vital skills as we need to negotiate every day with our friends, teachers and families (and even the dog!).

To download the student handouts and the PowerPoint slides for the lesson, please go to www.openup.co.uk/positivepsychology.

Lesson 34: Sweet Trading

HOW TO

Teacher Explanation (10 min.)

Teacher Discussion

This lesson will explore the basics of negotiation. Negotiation is one of life's essential skills as the students negotiate all day long with teachers, family, friends, siblings, etc. Indeed, the best negotiators in the world are children (who have the knack of perseverance and creativity!).

> Negotiation can be defined as the art of reaching an agreement between two or more parties (Kennedy 1997).

The lesson will involve an experiential exercise called 'Sweet Trading' that will last the whole lesson. The aim of the exercise is for the students to understand the basics of negotiation, including what it takes to achieve a win/win outcome in life. Building on Lessons 3 and 4, where the students explored assertion, confidence and collaboration, the principles of negotiation are further hallmarks of a confident person.

> Negotiation writers would add to this definition by explaining that a good negotiation only happens when both sides feel happy with the outcome. That is, both sides feel they have 'won' (Covey et al. 1989; Fisher et al. 1991).

The students are told that in a moment they will receive their brief for the game, which will also be read out aloud. They will also receive an outline for planning which needs to happen before trading needs can start.

In order to play the game, the teacher will need the sweet resource. 60 sweets are needed, ten types of six different sweets. As the scoring chart has been designed with specific sweets in mind, it would be useful for the teacher to have Éclairs, Penguins, Kit Kat, Twix, Snickers and Mars Bars. Randomly divide all these sweets into ten packs of six sweets.

The sweets must not be handed out at this stage.

Teacher Explanation (10 min.)

 Teacher Discussion and PowerPoint Presentation

The students are divided into ten teams, each of three people. Teacher reads out the attached brief with the students: this outlines the objective of the game, the rules of the game, how to score points, the grounds for disqualification and the timing.

Small children are brilliant negotiators, but primarily through strategies of perseverance, manipulation and high emotion! It is important for adolescents to learn this life skill and broaden their ability to reach win/win outcomes through planning, discussion, flexibility and positive relationships (Fisher et al. 1991; Forgas 1998).

After the brief has been read out, the teacher runs through the planning presentation on the PowerPoint. The five basic rules for negotiation highlighted on the presentation are as follows:

1. Make a plan (remember, failure to plan = plan to fail).

2. Plan your Best outcome, your Realistic outcome and your Walk-away (your lowest outcome at which you will walk away from the deal).

3. Create as many options as possible so that you can be flexible.

4. Give and Get (trade, don't just give stuff away).

5. Remember that behind every negotiation is a relationship. Be friendly and people are more likely to want to negotiate with you.

Class Activity 1: Planning Sweet Trading (10 min.)
Small Group Activity

The sweets are handed out (ideally in a brown paper bag) to each team. A random selection of six sweets should be given to each group.

'Sweet Trading' is based on an idea from the free training ideas website, www.businessballs.com. It has been built on and designed by MindSpring Ltd.

Teacher gives each team 10 minutes to make a plan. In this time they should look at their 'hand' (their sweet collection), look at some possible total values they could make, decide what their best and realistic options are and decide who they are going to start trading with.

No trading should happen in these 10 minutes.

Class Activity 2: Let the Trading Commence! (20 min.)
Small Group Activity

The students may now start trading for 15 minutes. As the students start to trade they should be having simple trades – one member of their team with another member from a different team. In each trade, the students (as per the brief) can offer to swap one or more sweets for one or more sweets from the other team. This may mean that a higher value sweet may be swapped for two or more lower value sweets.

Summary (10 min.)

Teacher-Led/Whole Class Discussion

Teacher asks the students to total up their scores. Their final points score is detailed on the scoring sheet on the Sweet Trading handout and is a combination of table 1 plus table 2 – that is, the value of each specific sweet coupled with the value of the 'hand'. Collect in the final points from each team.

> The concept of trust as the foundation of a positive relationship between adolescents is documented in Paul Martin's book *Making Happy People: The Nature of Happiness and its Origins in Childhood* (2006).

To help with scoring, here are some examples:

- Team A ends up with five Mars bars – these would be worth 50 points for the 5 of a kind, plus $5 \times 6 = 30$ points (as each Mars Bar is worth 6 points) making a total of 80 points.

- Team B ends up with 6 Éclairs – these would be worth 60 points for the 6 of a kind plus $6 \times 1 = 6$ points for the Éclairs, making a total of 66 points.

- Team C ends up with 3 Mars Bars and 3 Twix – these would be worth 38 for the hand plus 18 plus 12 making a total of 68 points.

> Scientist and writer Robert Cialdini highlights the need for 'reciprocity' (give and take) as a fundamental part of influencing other people (Cialdini 2006).

Furthermore, the teacher explores with students the following questions:

- Who feels they have won (and why?).

- It is perfectly possible for all teams to have an identical score (one sweet of each kind per team). This would equal a true win/win. Why did this not happen? (Assuming it has not happened, which is very rare.) This is a really important discussion to have, as, when competition is involved throughout life, people usually end up with a win/lose situation.

- What did they learn about negotiation?

- What has to be in place for a good negotiation to happen?

This brief discussion should cover the following three important points about negotiation:

1. It is very hard to achieve a true win/win. When competition is involved, we are psychologically driven to beat others.

2. A successful negotiation involves trust. Once trust is broken, it is unlikely that a win/win will be achieved.

3. Planning is very important in negotiation.

In summary, students are asked to tell teacher the areas in life where their negotiation skills are important and reiterate the importance of negotiation in developing a confident, assertive approach in life.

UNIT 6: POSITIVE RELATIONSHIPS

Lesson 35: Kindness and Gratitude

LESSON PLAN

Aims and Objectives	Resources
To appreciate the role of kindness and gratitude To explore random act of kindness To practise the gratitude diary and gratitude letters	Episodes from *Pay It Forward* Kindness and Gratitude Ideas handout My Thank You Letter handout What Went Well handout Computer with internet access

Teacher Explanation (5 min.)
Teacher-led Discussion/Reflective Questioning

● Students are asked to remember what the kindest thing someone ever did for them was.

● Teacher discusses some of these examples and how they made them feel.

Teacher Explanation: Kindness and Gratitude (20 min.)
Teacher Lecture/Movie/Song/Discussion

● The teacher introduces the story of *Pay it Forward*, playing some episodes from the movie.

● Everyone brainstorms what kind acts people can do for each other, using www.actsofkindness.org website as a prompt.

● Teacher introduces the notion of gratitude (appreciation, thankfulness) and discusses the various forms it can take.

● Everyone listens to the gratitude song.

Class Activity 1: Three Good Things (5 min.)
Small Group Activity

● In small groups of 4–5 everyone discusses three good things that happened to every member of the group yesterday.

● Help each other identify what their role in these good things was.

Class Activity 2: Thank You Letter (20 min.)

Individual Activity/Class Discussion

- Students Complete 'People I Am Grateful To' list on their handout.

- Students are asked to choose one of these people and write them a thank you letter.

- Everyone discusses together what they can do with this letter.

Summary and Homework: What Went Well (10 min.)

Teacher's Instructions

- The teacher introduces the instructions for the Gratitude Diary, asking students to complete it every night for one week.

- A possible extension of this lesson is to ask students to perform five acts of kindness in the next week.

To download the student handouts and the PowerPoint slides for the lesson, please go to www.openup.co.uk/positivepsychology.

Lesson 35: Kindness and Gratitude

HOW TO

Teacher Explanation (5 min.)
Teacher-led Discussion/Reflective Questioning

The teacher asks students to remember what the kindest thing someone ever did for them was. If they struggle to remember, the teacher suggests that it may be someone giving them an unexpected present, taking them somewhere or even rescuing them from a dangerous situation. The teacher may want to give an example from their own life. Teacher discusses some of these examples, highlighting also how they made them feel. Then the Kindness and Gratitude Ideas handout is introduced as the last relationship skill to be learnt. Teacher checks if everyone understands what these words mean.

Teacher Explanation: Kindness and Gratitude (20 min.)
Teacher Lecture/Movie/Song/Discussion

The teacher introduces the story of *Pay it Forward*, playing some episodes from the movie (there are a selection of clips on YouTube). Students are asked how the main character's behaviour can be described, with regard to the tramp, his mother, his teacher and his friend. Have students come across any situation when a kind act gave rise to more kindness? The teacher might want to consider what may prevent and facilitate people implementing the principle suggested in the movie.

> The ending of the movie may be disturbing (the character's death), so you may not want to show it.

Kindness is about showing care, love and affection towards another person, not for the sake of what we will get out of it, but for the sake of what they will get out of it. The focus on the other is essential here; kindness should not be confused with niceness, which is a type of behaviour that is primarily beneficial for the bearer.

> Researchers suggest a number of reasons why doing kind acts for others make people happier. They make one feel more confident, in control and optimistic about their ability to make a difference. They enable one to connect with other people. They also make us feel more positive about other people and the community one lives in, thus fostering co-operation (Lyubomirsky et al. 2005b).

The beauty of kindness is that it has an effect on both the receiver and the giver, so it's a brilliant win/win scenario. Kind people are generally happier and healthier. Everyone brainstorms together what kind acts people can do for each other, using www.actsofkindness.org website as a prompt. Students are to record some of these ideas on their handouts. The teacher may want to implement some suggestions from the website for their school life. One beautiful exercise is called the Kindness Catcher and involves writing the name of anyone 'caught' being kind and their action on Post-it notes and placing them in a jar that is opened at the end of the week.

> This exercise is further described in *Celebrating Strengths* by Fox Eades (2008).

At this point the teacher can introduce gratitude as a common response to kindness. Gratitude appears to be an emotion which many people feel frequently and strongly. All major world religions – Judaism, Christianity, Islam, Hinduism and Buddhism – emphasize its importance. The Buddha stated that thankfulness is a core aspect of a noble person. The philosopher Cicero said that gratitude is the greatest of all virtues and the parent of all the others.

> Lyubomirsky (2007) states that expressing gratitude is a form of meta-strategy for achieving happiness. Emmons (2007) has also found that the expression of gratitude is associated with happiness, well-being, physical exercise, life satisfaction, optimism, forgiveness, enthusiasm and love. Polak and McCullough (2006) state that gratitude alleviates materialistic striving which is associated with negative effects. In fact, Emmons (2007) goes as far as to state that if we express gratitude as a way of life, we can increase our happiness set point by 25 per cent.

Gratitude is a continuum from politely saying thank you when given a gift at one end, to living a life of gratefulness at the other end. The term gratitude itself comes from the Latin 'gratia' meaning grace. Some scholars describe is as a felt sense of wonder, thankfulness and appreciation for life.

In other words, gratitude is about not taking life for granted. Jenny Fox Eades (2008, p. 147) says: 'It includes the capacity to notice and wonder at the ordinary – clean water in our taps, at the colours of the spring, at a kind word – and to take nothing for granted.'

Gratitude operates in terms of being grateful to someone, being grateful to life for something, being grateful to a person for something in particular or the tendency to experience gratitude as ongoing across situations. This means that gratitude can be directed to someone (to whom we can actually express it), or just cultivated within oneself (without necessarily involving others).

Finally, students listen to the gratitude song from: http://www.youtube.com/watch?v=2bf1akDYakw (or type 'the gratitude song' into YouTube).

Class Activity 1: Three Good Things (5 min.)
Small Group Activity

In small groups of 4–5, the teacher asks students to discuss three good things that happened to every member of the group yesterday. These can be significant or relatively unimportant events, it doesn't matter. For each thing, everyone reflects on why it went well. Students might need to help one another identify what their role in these good things was.

> Probably the most powerful of all positive psychology techniques, different variants of this exercise (counting blessing, being thankful, what went well) have been investigated by several researchers, always with substantial results. It has been found to lastingly increase happiness and decrease depressive symptoms for up to six months. (Seligman et al. 2005)

Class Activity 2: Thank You Letter (20 min.)
Individual Activity/Class Discussion

Teacher asks the students to complete 'People I Am Grateful To' list on their 'Kindness and Ideas' handout then asks them to choose one of these people and write them a Thank You Letter, (handout online) giving them instructions below:

> This is another exercise that has been tested experimentally. It increases well-being and positive emotions substantially in the aftermath of the event, although the changes do wear off eventually. (Seligman et al. 2005)

Write a gratitude letter. Think of someone who has been particularly kind to you, or helped you in some way, to whom you have never expressed your thanks. It might be a parent, friend, relative or teacher. Write them a letter, describing specifically what they did and what effect it had on you and your life. Try to include concrete examples of what the recipient has done. Try to explain how the recipient influenced you. You may want to discuss how your life would have been different without this person's role in it.

Once students have finished writing, the teacher discusses the following questions with them:

- What helped them choose the person to whom they wanted to express gratitude?

- What did it feel like to write this letter? Did it flow or was it hard to do?

- What would they like to do with this letter now?

The last point should be considered carefully, emphasizing that students may want to make different choices. They may choose to deliver this letter in person and read it out to the benefactor, or simply wait until they have read it. They may want to send the letter or may do nothing. The teacher discusses some possible implications of all these choices.

> The original form (and therefore findings) of this exercise are based on the option of delivering the letter and reading it out loud. However, these instructions may not always be appropriate for British students.

Summary and Homework: What Went Well (10 min.)

Teacher's Instructions

The instructions for this exercise are fairly straightforward, as it is very similar to the one performed in the class.

> Every night for one week, look back at your day just before you go to bed and find three things that went well for you during the day. Write them down and reflect on your role in them.

A possible homework extension activity. This exercise needs to be performed on one day with five acts of kindness done during a single day. As the name suggests, this intervention is about doing something good for another human being. This may be large or small, but the act needs to benefit them in some way. Options can range from helping mum to do the dishes to taking a neighbour's dog for a walk, or visiting one's elderly auntie. In our age of social networking sites, the opportunities for small touches are practically endless. Students may send someone a Growing Gift on Facebook (a flower that is hidden at first but comes to bloom within a few days) or a thoughtful e-card.

> Not only do random acts of kindness make other people feel better, they also increase the happiness of the giver, especially if several acts are carried out on the same day. It is also important to vary these acts so that they remain fresh and meaningful. (Lyubomirsky 2007)

UNIT 6: POSITIVE RELATIONSHIPS

Lesson 36: Happiness across Cultures

LESSON PLAN

Aims and Objectives	Resources
To understand why and how countries differ in happiness To discuss happiness in Britain today	PowerPoint Lesson 36 *Happiness Formula* website Happiness map Slide show from *Business Week* Happiness Manifesto handout PCs with internet access

Teacher Explanation (5 min.)

Teacher Discussion

- The teacher points out that nations differ quite substantially in their happiness levels.

Class Activity 1: How Happy is Your Country? (25 min.)

Small Group Activity

- In small groups of 5–6, students prepare a case to justify a ranking of a country (allocated), using some basic facts provided and internet research.

- Students decorate this country's flag.

Class Activity 2: Happiness Debate (20 min.)

Students' Presentations/PowerPoint Lecture/Reflective Questioning

- Students present their arguments for the ranking order of their country.

- The teacher introduces the actual ranking based on White's (2007) study.

- Teacher discusses the reasons for these positions (differences in wealth, health and education).

- Teacher explains why having income sufficient to satisfy basic needs is so important.

- Teacher introduces the diminishing effects of more income and why there are still significant differences between wealthy countries (Denmark vs. Britain).

- The concept of Affluenza is discussed.

- All is concluded with a slide show on the ten happiest countries and the world happiness map.

- If some time remains, the teacher may consider showing an episode from the *Happiness Formula* on Bhutan, one of the world's happiest countries.

Teacher Explanation: Happiness in Britain Today (5 min.)
PowerPoint Lecture/Reflective Questioning

- Teacher discusses the slight decline in happiness level in Britain.

- Teacher discusses some possible reasons behind the decline.

Summary and Homework: A Happiness Manifesto (5 min.)
Teacher's Instructions

- Students need to write a happiness manifesto with the aim of advising the British government on how to increase happiness in this country.

To download the student handouts and the PowerPoint slides for the lesson, please go to www.openup.co.uk/positivepsychology.

HOW TO

Teacher Explanation (5 min.)
Teacher Discussion

Nations differ quite substantially with regard to their happiness levels. What is interesting is that some things that make little difference to individuals' well-being are at play for nations.

Class Activity 1: How Happy is Your Country? (25 min.)
Small Group Activity

Teacher divides the class into five small groups and allocates one of the five different countries to each of the groups. Teacher explains that their task is to decide on the order of these countries with regard to happiness (1–5) and to defend their group's decision.

> White's (2007) research is a meta-analysis of over 100 different studies on happiness across cultures, involving more than 80,000 people.

Each group has 25 minutes, during which they also have to decorate a flag (which can be downloaded from the internet). The teacher reads through some of the basic facts provided (see below). (Facts accurate at the time of writing.) Students carry out further research on the internet, make a decision and formulate their case.

The UK

- Primary and secondary education is free, while university education is not.
- Rich history.
- 5 per cent of the population is unemployed.
- Average life expectancy is 81 years for women and 76 years for men.
- Free healthcare.
- Culture that is tolerant of all nations.

The USA

- 5.5 per cent of the population is unemployed.
- Average life expectancy is 79 years for women and 73 years for men.
- Large divide between rich and poor.

- Lots of nationalities living together, but a lot of racial tension.

- Opportunities for all.

- Healthcare is good if you can afford it (no state healthcare).

- Huge variety of scenery.

Russia

- 6 per cent of the population is unemployed.

- Average life expectancy is 72 years for women and 59 years for men.

- Very good healthcare.

- The country is moving from the communist to the capitalist system.

- High levels of corruption and crime.

Zimbabwe

- Very hot climate.

- Lots of interesting animals.

- Great scenery.

- 25 per cent of the population have AIDS.

- Average life expectancy is 34 years for women and 37 years for men.

- 80 per cent of people are unemployed.

Denmark

- A Scandinavian country with quite cold weather.

- Exceptionally high taxes.

- 3 per cent of the population is unemployed.

- All education is free.

- Many leisure facilities are free.

- Average life expectancy is 80 years for women and 76 years for men.

Class Activity 2: Happiness Debate (20 min.)

Students' Presentations/PowerPoint Lecture/Reflective Questioning

Students present their arguments for the ranking order of their country (out of five possible). The actual ranking order in accordance to research by Adrian White (2007) is:

1. Denmark (1st out of 178 countries)

2. USA (23rd out of 178 countries)

3. UK (41st out of 178 countries)

4. Russia (167th out of 178 countries)

5. Zimbabwe (177th out of 178 countries)

Teacher discusses why these countries may be occupying these positions. Research shows that a nation's level of happiness is closely associated with its state of wealth, health and education (White 2007). As we know, income is linked to satisfaction of basic biological needs (e.g., food, shelter). Furthermore, wealthier countries have social welfare programmes to protect against adverse effects of poverty. Wealthier countries also have more human rights, lower crime, more democracy, better literacy and better life expectancy. However, money is not everything. Research shows that once income reaches £10, 000 per person, more money is not going to make a country any happier. In most developed countries, income increased up to four times in the past 50 years, but happiness levels stayed the same.

Why is that? First of all, huge differences between the rich and the poor are counter-productive for happiness. This is why Denmark (where citizens have to pay a lot of taxes and the differences between citizens are small) is so much happier than the US and the UK, where taxes are lower and the differences are large. Second, research shows that happy people place a high value on love, while unhappy people place a high value on money (Diener and Oishi 2000). Countries in which the acquisition of wealth is highly valued have higher materialistic attitudes, more competitiveness and less time for socializing and leisure. This is a phenomenon known as Affluenza virus (James 2007).

The teacher concludes this exercise with a slide show on the ten happiest countries from the *Business Week* article Rating Countries for the Happiness Factor, available at:

www.businessweek.com/globalbiz/content/oct2006/gb20061011_072596.htm.
Teacher can also show the world happiness map, available at:

http://news.bbc.co.uk/1/hi/5224306.stm. (Or type BBC world happiness map into Google).

If there is some extra time, the teacher may want to show students an episode from the *Happiness Formula* on Bhutan, one of the world's happiest countries:

http://news.bbc.co.uk/1/hi/programmes/happiness_formula/

Teacher Explanation: Happiness in Britain Today (5 min.)
Teacher-led PowerPoint Lecture/Reflective Questioning

So how is Britain doing with regard to happiness? Well, it has been quite a happy country for the past 50 years, and it still doing OK at the moment, being in the 41st place out of 178 countries. However, there are also some indications that British happiness levels are declining. In the 1950s, 52 per cent of the population were very happy, while now only 36 per cent say the same. Further information on the British levels of happiness can be found on the Happiness formula website, available at:

http://news.bbc.co.uk/1/hi/programmes/happiness_formula/4771908.stm.

Summary and Homework: A Happiness Manifesto (5 min.)

Teacher's Instructions

Students are asked to imagine that they have a chance to advise the government on how to increase happiness in Britain. They need to write a concise (no more than seven points) Happiness Manifesto to the government on the handouts provided.

References

Andrews, G., Szabó, M. and Burns, J. (2001) *Avertable Risk Factors for Depression*. Report for BeyondBlue, the Australian National Depression Initiative.

Andrews, G., Szabo, M. and Burns, J. (2002) Preventing major depression in young people. *British Journal of Psychiatry*, 181: 460–2.

Arey, B. and Beal, M. (2002) The role of exercise in the prevention and treatment of wasting in AIDS. *Journal of the Association of Nurses in AIDS Care*, 13(1): 29–49.

Argyle, M. (2001) *The Psychology of Happiness*. Hove: Routledge.

Babyak, M., Blumenthal, J.A., Herman, S., Khatri, P., Doraiswamy, M. and Moore, K. et al. (2000) Exercise treatment for major depression: maintenance of therapeutic benefit at ten months. *Psychosomatic Medicine*, 62(5): 633–8.

Baer, R.A. (2003) Mindfulness training as a clinical intervention. *Clinical Psychology: Science and Practice*, 10(2).

Bandura, A. (1997) *Self-efficacy: The Exercise of Control*. New York: Worth Publishers.

Bassi, M. and Della Fave, A. (2004) Adolescence and the changing context of optimal experience in time: Italy,1986–2000. *Journal of Happiness Studies*, 5: 155–79.

Baumeister, R., Campbell, J.D., Krueger, J.I. and Vohs, K.D. (2003) Does high self-esteem cause better performance, interpersonal success, happiness or healthier lifestyles? *Psychological Science in the Public Interest*, 4(1): 1–44.

Baumeister, R., Finkenhauer, C. and Vohs, K.D. (2001) Bad is stronger than good. *Review of General Psychology*, 5: 323–37.

Baylis, N. and Morris, I. (2006) *Wellington College: The Skills of Well-being: Course Overview*. Tonbridge Wells: Wellington College.

Beck, A.T., Rush, A.J., Shaw, B.F. and Emery, D. (1979) *Cognitive Therapy of Depression*. New York: Guilford Press.

Benard, B. (2004) *Resiliency: What We Have Learned*. San Francisco: WestEd.

Benson, M. (1998) *The Relaxation Response*. New York: Avon Books.

Bernstein, D.A. and Borkovec, T.D. (1973) *Progressive Relaxation Training: A Manual for the Helping Profession*. Champaign, IL: Research Press.

Biswas-Diener, R. and Diener, E. (2001) Making the best of a bad situation: satisfaction in the slums of Calcutta. *Social Indicators Research*, 55: 329–52.

Boniwell, I. (2006) *Positive Psychology in a Nutshell*. London: PWBC.

Boniwell, I. and Zimbardo, P.G. (2004) Balancing time perspective in pursuit of optimal functioning. In P.A. Linley and S. Joseph (eds) *Positive Psychology in Practice*. Hoboken, NJ: John Wiley & Sons, pp. 165–78.

Boniwell, I. and Osin, E. (in preparation) Validation of a well-being curriculum for Y7 and Y10 school students in the Haberdasher's Aske's Federation.

Boniwell, I., Ryan, L., Tunariu, A. and Hefferon, K. (in preparation) Development and validation of a SPARK Resilience Curriculum for secondary school students.

Bower, S.A. and Bower, G. (1991) *Asserting Yourself: A Guide to Positive Change*. New York: Da Capo Press.

Brand, S., Felner, R., Shim, M., Seitsinger, A. and Dumas, T. (2003) Middle school improvement and reform: development and validation of a school-level assessment of climate, cultural pluralism and school safety. *Journal of Educational Psychology*, 95: 570–88.

Brickman, P., Coates, D. and Janoff-Bulman, R. (1978) Lottery winners and accident victims: is happiness relative? *Journal of Personality and Social Psychology*, 36(8): 917–27.

Brown, K. and Ryan, R. (2003) The benefits of being present: mindfulness and its role in psychological well-being. *Journal of Personality and Social Psychology*, 84: 822–48.

Brunwasser, S.M., Gillham, J.E. and Kim, E.S. (2009) A meta-analytic review of the Penn Resiliency Program's effect on depressive symptoms. *Journal of Consulting and Clinical Psychology*, 77(6): 1042–54.

Bryant, F.B. (2003) Savouring Beliefs Inventory (SBI): a scale for measuring beliefs about savouring. *Journal of Mental Health*, 12(2): 175–96.

Bryant, F.B., Smart, C.M. and King, S.P. (2005) Using the past to enhance the presence: boosting happiness through positive reminiscence. *Journal of Happiness Studies*, 6: 227–60.

Bryant, F.B. and Veroff, J. (2006) *Savoring: A New Model of Positive Experience*. Mahwah, NJ: Lawrence Erlbaum.

Buckingham, M. and Coffman, C. (1999) *First, Break All the Rules: What the World's Greatest Managers Do Differently*. New York: Simon & Schuster.

Cameron, R.J. and Maginn, C. (manuscript submitted for publication) The authentic warmth dimension of professional childcare.

Carmody, J. and Baer, R.A.K. (2008) Relationships between mindfulness practice and levels of mindfulness, medical and psychological symptoms and well-being in a mindfulness-based stress reduction program. *Journal of Behavioral Medicine*, 31: 23–33.

Carr, A. (2004) *Positive Psychology*. Hove and New York: Brunner-Routledge.

Carver, C.S. and Scheier, M.F. (2002) Optimism. In C.R. Snyder and S.J. Lopez (eds) *Handbook of Positive Psychology*. New York: Oxford University Press, pp. 231–43.

CASEL (Collaboration for Academic and Social-Emotional Learning) (2010), www.casel.org (accessed 11 February 2011).

Catalano, R.F., Haggerty, K.P., Oesterle, S., Fleming, C.B. and Hawkins, J.D. (2003) The importance of bonding to school for healthy development: Findings from the Social Development Research Group, paper presented at Wingspread Conference on School Connectedness. Racine, WI.

Cialdini, R. (2006) *Influence: The Science of Persuasion*. New York: HarperCollins.

Claxton, G. (1998) *Hare Brain, Tortoise Mind*. London: Fourth Estate.

Clifton, D.O. and Anderson, E.C. (2001) *StrengthsQuest*. Washington, DC: The Gallup Organisation.

Cloninger, C.R. (2004) *Feeling Good: The Science of Well-being*. New York: Oxford University Press.

Collins, J. and Porras, J. (1996) Building your company's vision, *Harvard Business Review*, 74(5): 65–77.

Corbin, C. (1972) *Ergogenic Aids and Muscular Performance*. New York: Academic Press.

Covey, L.S., Glassman, A.H. and Stetner, F. (1989) Cigarette smoking and major depression. *Journal of Addictive Diseases*, 17: 35–46.

Covey, S. (1989) *The 7 Habits of Highly Effective People*. London: Simon & Schuster.

Craig, C. (2007) *Creating Confidence*. Glasgow: Centre for Confidence and Well Being.

Csikszentmihalyi, M. (1998) *Living Well: The Psychology of Everyday Life*. New York: Phoenix.

Csikszentmihalyi, M. (2000) *Beyond Boredom and Anxiety: Experiencing Flow in Work and Play*. San Francisco: Jossey-Bass.

Csikszentmihalyi, M. (2002) *Flow*. London: Random House.

Csikszentmihalyi, M. and Csikszentmihalyi, I. (1988) *Optimal Experience: Psychological Studies of Flow in Consciousness*. Cambridge: Cambridge University Press.

Csikszentmihalyi, M., Rathunde, K. and Whalen, S. (1996) *Talented Teenagers*. Cambridge: Cambridge University Press.

Curry, L.A., Snyder, C.R. and Cook, D.L. (1997) Role of hope in academic and sport achievement. *Journal of Personality and Social Psychology*, 73(6): 1257–67.

Danish, S.J. (1996) Going for the goal: a life-skills program for adolescents. In G.W. Abele and T.P. Gullotta (eds) *Primary Prevention Works*. Newbury Park, CA: Sage.

Danner, D., Snowdon, D. and Friesen, W. (2001) Positive emotions early in life and the longevity: findings from the nun study. *Journal of Personality and Social Psychology*, 80, 804–13.

Davidson, R.J. (2003) Alterations in brain and immune function produced by mindfulness meditation. *Psychosomatic Medicine*, 65: 564–70.

DCSF (2007) *Children and Young People Today: Evidence to Support the Children's Plan*. London: Department for Children, Schools and Families.

De Bono, E. (1970) *Lateral Thinking: Creativity Step by Step*. New York: Harper & Row.

DfES (2005) *Excellence and Enjoyment: Social and Emotional Aspects of Learning Guidance*. London: Department for Education and Skills.

DfES (2007a) *Social and Emotional Aspects of Learning for Secondary Schools (SEAL): Guidance Booklet*. London: TSO.

DfES (2007b) *The Children's Plan: Building Brighter Futures*. Available at: www.dfes.gov.uk/publications/childrensplan/.

Diener, E. and Biswas-Diener, R. (2002) Will money increase subjective well-being? A literature review and guide to needed research. *Social Indicators Research*, 57: 119–69.

Diener, E., Diener, M. and Diener, C. (1995) Factors predicting the subjective well-being of nations. *Journal of Personality and Social Psychology*, 69: 851–64.

Diener, E., Lucas, E.L. and Oishi, S. (2001) Subjective well-being. In C.R. Snyder and S.J. Lopez (eds) *Handbook of Positive Psychology*. New York: Oxford University Press.

Diener, E. and Oishi, S. (2000) Money and happiness: income and subjective well-being.across nations. In E. Diener and E.M. Suh (eds) *Culture and Subjective Well-being*. Cambridge, MA: MIT Press, pp. 185–218.

Dimidjian, S. and Linehan, M. M. (2003) Defining an agenda for future research on the clinical application of mindfulness practice. *Clinical Psychology: Science and Practice*, 10: 166–71.

Dinges, D. (2007) Effects of sleep disorders and sleep restriction. *Behavioural Sleep Medicine*, 5(2): 79–82.

Dion, K. and Berscheid, E. (1974) Physical attractiveness and peer perception among children. *Sociometry*, 37(1): 1–12.

Dion, K., Berscheid, E. and Walster, E. (1974) What is beautiful is good. *Journal of Personality and Social Psychology*, 24: 285–90.

Dix, K.L., Owens, S. and Spears, B. (2009) *KidsMatter Evaluation Executive Summary.* Available at: www.kidsmatter.edu.au/wp/wp-content/uploads/2009/10/kidsmatter-executive-summary (accessed 10 January 2011).

Dobkin, P.L. and Zhao, Q. (2011) Increased mindfulness: the active component of the mindfulness-based stress reduction program? *Complementary Therapies in Clinical Practice*, 17: 22–7.

Dryfoos, J.G. (1990) *Adolescents at Risks: Prevalence and Prevention.* New York: Oxford University Press.

Duckworth, A.L. and Seligman, M.E.P. (2005) Self-discipline outdoes IQ in predicting academic performance of adolescents. *Psychological Science*, 16(12): 939–44.

Dunbar, R. (2005) *The Human Story.* London: Faber & Faber.

Durlak, J.A. and Wells, A.M. (1997) Primary prevention mental health programs for children and adolescents: a meta-analytic review. *American Journal of Community Psychology*, 25(2): 115–52.

Dweck, C.S. (2006) *Mindset: The New Psychology of Success.* New York: Random House.

Eades, J. (2008) *Celebrating Strengths: Building Strengths-based Schools.* Warwick: CAPP Press.

Eckert, T.L. and Hinze, J.M. (2000) Behavioral conceptions and applications of acceptability: issues related to service delivery and research methodology. *School Psychology Quarterly*, 15: 123–48.

Ekman, P. (1999) Basic emotions. In T. Dalgleish and M. Power (eds) *Handbook of Cognition and Emotion.* Chichester: John Wiley & Sons.

Elliott, S.N., Witt, J.C. and Kratochwill, T.R. (1991) Selecting, implementing and evaluating classroom interventions. In G. Stoner, M.R. Shinn and H.M. Walker (eds) *Interventions for Achievement and Behavior Problems.* Silver Springs, MD: National Association of School Psychologists, pp. 99–135.

Emler, N. (2003) Does it matter if young people have low self esteem? In K. Richards (ed.) *Self-esteem and Youth Development.* Ambleside: Brathay Hall Trust, pp. 1–26.

Emmons, R. (2007) *Thanks! How the New Science of Gratitude Can Make You Happier.* New York: Houghton-Mifflin.

Fisher, R., Ury, W. and Patton, B. (1991) *Getting to Yes: Negotiating Agreement Without Giving In.* New York: Penguin.

Fontana, D. and Slack, I. (1997) *Teaching Meditation to Children: The Practical Guide to the Use and Benefits of Meditation Techniques.* Boston, MA: Element.

Ford, M.E. and Nichols, C.W. (1991) Using goals assessment to identify motivational patterns and facilitate behavioural regulation and achievement. *Advances in Motivation and Achievement*, 7: 51–84.

Forgas, J.P. (1998) On feeling good and getting your way: mood effects on negotiator cognition and behavior. *Journal of Personality and Social Psychology*, 74: 565–77.

Fox Eades, J. (2008) *Celebrating Strengths: Building Strengths-based Schools.* Warwick: CAPP Press.

Fredrickson, B.L. (1998) What good are positive emotions? *Review of General Psychology*, 2: 300–19.

Fredrickson, B.L. (2001) The role of positive emotions in positive psychology: The broaden-and-build theory of positive emotions. *American Psychologist*, 56: 218–26.

Fredrickson, B.L. (2002) Positive emotions. In C.R. Snyder and S.J. Lopez (eds) *Handbook of Positive Psychology.* New York: Oxford University Press, pp.120–34.

Gable, S.L., Reis, H.T., Asher, E.R. and Impett, E.A. (2004) What do you do when things go right? The intrapersonal and interpersonal benefits of sharing positive events, *Journal of Personality and Social Psychology*, 87: 228–45.

Gallwey, W.T. (1975) *The Inner Game of Tennis.* London: Pan Books.

Gardner, H. (1983) *Frames of Mind: The Theory of Multiple Intelligences.* New York: Basic Books.

Gardner, H. (1999) *Intelligence Reframed: Multiple Intelligences for the 21st century.* New York: Basic Books.

Garrison, C.Z., Schluchter, M.D., Schoenbach, V.J. and Kaplan, B.K. (1989) Epidemiology of depressive symptoms in young adolescents. *Journal of the American Academy of Child and Adolescent Psychiatry*, 28: 343–51.

Gilani, T. and Boniwell, I. (in preparation) The Well-being Curriculum: a comprehensive, evidence-based programme for primary school children.

Gillham, J.E., Reivich, K.J. and Freres, D.R. (2007) School based prevention of depressive symptoms: a randomized controlled study of the effectiveness and specificity of the Penn Resiliency Program. *Journal of Consulting and Clinical Psychology*, 75(1): 9–19.

Goleman, D. (1996) *Emotional Intelligence: Why It Can Matter More Than IQ.* New York: Bantam Books.

Goleman, D. (2003) *Destructive Emotions.* London: Bantam Books.

Govindji, R. and Linley, P. A. (2007) Strengths use, self-concordance and well-being: implications for strengths coaching and coaching psychologists. *International Coaching Psychology Review*, 2(2): 143–53.

Greco, L.A., Blackledge, J.T., Coyne, L.W. and Ehrenreich, J. (2005) Integrating acceptance and mindfulness into treatments for child and adolescent anxiety disorders. In S.M. Orsillo and L. Roemer (eds) *Acceptance and Mindfulness-Based Approaches to Anxiety Conceptualization and Treatment.* New York: Springer.

Green, H., McGinnity, A., Meltzer, H., Ford, T. and Goodman, R. (2005) *Mental Health of Children and Young People in Great Britain 2004.* London: Office for National Statistics.

Greenberg, M.T., Domitrovich, C. and Bumbarger, B. (2001) *Preventing Mental Disorders in School-Age Children: A Review of the Effectiveness of Prevention Programs.* Washington, DC: Center for Mental Health Services (CMHS), Substance Abuse Mental Health Services Administration, US Department of Health and Human Services.

Greenberg, M., Weissberg, R., O'Brien, M., Zins, J., Fredericks, L., Resnik, H. et al. (2003) Enhancing school-based prevention and youth development through coordinated social, emotional and academic learning. *American Psychologist,* 58: 466–74.

Gresham, F.M. and Lopez, M.F. (1996) Social validation: a unifying concept for school-based consultation. *School Psychology Quarterly,* 11: 204–27.

Hamilton, N.A., Gallagher, M.W. and Preacher, K.J. (2007a) Insomnia and well-being. *Journal of Consulting and Clinical Psychology,* 75(6): 939–46.

Hamilton, N.A., Nelson, C., Stevens, N. and Kitzman, H. (2007b) Sleep and psychological well-being. *Social Indicators Research,* 82: 147–63.

Hassmen, P., Koivula, N. and Uutela, A. (2000) Physical exercise and psychological well-being: a population study in Finland. *Preventive Medicine,* 30(1): 17–25.

Hattie, J. (2003) *Teachers Make a Difference: What Is the Research Evidence?* Canberra: Australian Council for Educational Research.

Hattie, J. (2009) *Visible Learning: A Synthesis of Over 800 Meta-analyses Relating to Achievement.* London: Routledge.

Henry, J. (ed.) (2001) *Creative Management,* 2nd edn. London: Sage.

Henry, J. and Mayle, D.T. (eds) (2002) *Managing Innovation and Change,* 2nd edn. London: Sage.

Hodges, T.D. and Clifton, D.O. (2004) Strengths-based development in practice. In P.A. Linley and S. Joseph (eds) *Positive Psychology in Practice.* Hoboken, NJ: John Wiley & Sons, pp. 256–68.

Hooker, K. and Fodor, I. (2008) Teaching mindfulness to children. *Gestalt Review,* 12(1): 75–91.

Humphrey, A., Kalambouka, A., Bolton, J., Lendrum, A., Wigelsworth, M., Lennie, C. et al. (2008) *Primary Social and Emotional Aspects of Learning (SEAL): Evaluation of Small Group Work.* Available at: http://www.dcsf.gov.uk/research/data/uploadfiles/DCSF-RB064.pdf (accessed 11 February 2011).

James, O. (2007) *Affluenza.* London: Vermilion.

Judge, T.A. and Hurst, C. (2007) Capitalizing on one's advantage: role of core self-evaluations. *Journal of Applied Psychology,* 92: 1212–27.

Kabat-Zinn, J. (1994) *Wherever You Go, There You Are.* New York: Hyperion.

Kabat-Zinn J. (2003) Mindfulness-based interventions in context: past, present and future. *Clinical Psychology Science and Practice,* 10: 144–56.

Kabat-Zinn, J. (2005) *Coming to Our Senses.* New York: Hyperion.

Kahne, J. (1996) The politics of self-esteem. *American Education Research Journal,* 33: 3–22.

Kansas State University (2009) Popular songs can cue specific memories, psychology research shows. *Science Daily,* January 21. Available at: http:// www.sciencedaily.com/releases/2009/01/090121174126/htm.

Kasser, T. and Ryan, R.M. (1993) The dark side of the American Dream: correlates of financial success as a central life aspiration. *Journal of Personality and Social Psychology,* 65: 410–22.

Kasser, T. and Ryan, R.M. (1996) Further examining the American dream: differential correlates of intrinsic and extrinsic goals. *Personality and Social Psychology Bulletin,* 22: 280–7.

Keller, M. and Wood, P. (1989) Development of friendship reasoning: a study of interindividual differences in intraindividual change. *Developmental Psychology,* 25: 820–6.

Kellerman, A.L., Fuqua-Whitley, D.S., Rivara, F.P. and Mervy, J. (1998) Preventing youth violence: what works? *Annual Review of Public Health,* 19: 271–92.

Kennedy, G. (1997) *Everything is Negotiable.* London: Arrow Books.

King, L.A. (2001) The health benefits of writing about life goals. *Personality and Social Psychology Bulletin,* 27: 798–807.

King, L.A. and Napa, C.K. (1998) What makes a life good? *Journal of Personality and Social Psychology,* 75: 156–65.

Kritz-Silverstein, D., Barrett-Connor, E. and Corbeau, C. (2001) Cross-sectional and prospective study of exercise and depressed mood in the elderly: the Rancho Bernardo study. *American Journal of Epidemiology,* 153(6): 596–603.

Kubitz, K.A., Landers, D.M., Petruzzello, S.J. and Han, M. (1996) The effects of acute and chronic exercise on sleep: a meta-analytic review. *Sports Med,* 21(4): 277–91.

Langer, E. (2009) *Counter Clockwise.* New York: Random House.

Langlois, J.H., Kalakanis, L., Rubenstein, A.J., Larson, A., Hallam, M. and Smoot, M. (2000) Maxims or myths of beauty? A meta-analytic and theoretical review. *Psychological Bulletin.* 126: 390–423.

LaPorta, L.D. (2009) Twitter and YouTube: unexpected consequences of the self-esteem movement? *Psychiatric Times,* 26(11): 1–6.

Legros, M. (2009) *Child Poverty and Child Well-Being in the European Union: Policy Overview and Policy Impact Analysis. A Case Study: France.* Paris: EHESP School of Public Health.

Lennings, C.J. (1996) Self-efficacy and temporal orientation as predictors of treatment outcome in severely dependent alcoholics. *Alcoholism Treatment Quarterly*, 14: 71–9.

LeShan, L. (1974) *How to Meditate: A Guide to Self-Discovery.* New York: Bantam Books.

Lewinsohn, P.M., Hops, H., Roberts, R. and Seeley, J. (1993) Adolescent psychopathology: I. Prevalence and incidence of depression and other DSM-III-R disorders in high school students. *Journal of Abnormal Psychology*, 102: 110–20.

Linley, A. (2008) *From Average to A+.* Warwick: CAPP Press.

Linley, P.A. and Govindji, R. (2008) An evaluation of celebrating strengths. Unpublished manuscript.

Locke, E.A., Shaw, K.N., Saari, L.M. and Latham, G.P. (1981) Goal setting and task performance, 1969–1980. *Psychological Bulletin*, 90(1): 125–52.

Loehr, J. and Schwartz, T. (2003) *The Power of Full Engagement.* New York: Free Press.

Loewen, S. (2003) Variation in the frequency and characteristics of incidental focus on form. *Language Teaching Research*, 7: 315–45.

Lopez, S.J., Snyder, C.R., Magyar-Moe, J.L., Edwards, L.M., Pedrotti, J.T., Janowski, K. et al. (2004) Strategies for accentuating hope. In. P.A. Linley and S. Joseph (eds) *Positive Psychology in Practice.* Hoboken, NJ: John Wiley & Sons, pp. 388–404.

Luria, A.R. (1968) *The Mind of a Mnemonist.* New York: Basic Books.

Lyubomirsky, S. (2001) Why are some people happier than others? The role of cognitive and motivational processes in well-being. *American Psychologist*, 56(3): 239–49.

Lyubomirsky, S. (2007) *The How of Happiness.* London: Sphere.

Lyubomirsky, S., King, L. and Diener, E. (2005a) The benefits of frequent positive affect: does happiness lead to success? *Psychological Bulletin*, 131: 803–55.

Lyubomirsky, S., Sheldon, K. M. and Schkade, D. (2005b) Pursuing happiness: the architecture of sustainable change. *Review of General Psychology*, 9(2): 111–31.

Lyubomirsky, S., Sousa, L. and Dickerhoof, R (2006) The costs and benefits of writing, talking and thinking about life's triumphs and defeats. *Journal of Personality and Social Psychology*, 90(4): 692–708.

Mackay, I. (1984) *A Guide to Listening.* London: Gwynne Printers Ltd.

Martens, R. (1982) Imagery in sport. Paper presented at the Medical and Scientific Aspects of Elitism in Sport Conference, Brisbane, Australia.

Martin, J. (2000) *Technique Library.* Milton Keynes: Open University Press.

Martin, P. (2006) *Making Happy People: The Nature of Happiness and Its Origins in Childhood.* London: Harper Perennial.

Martin, R.A. (2001) Humour, laughter and physical health: methodological issues and research findings. *Psychological Bulletin*, 127: 504–19.

Martin, R.A. (2007) *The Psychology of Humour: An Integrative Approach.* Burlington, MA: Elsevier Academic Press.

Marzano, R.J., Pickering, D.J. and Pollock, J.E. (2001) *Classroom Instruction That Works: Research-Based Strategies for Increasing Student Achievement.* Alexandria, VA: Association for Supervision and Curriculum Development.

McCullough, E. (2001) *Forgiveness: Theory, Research and Practice.* New York: Guilford Press.

McCullough, M.E., Emmons, R.A. and Tsang, J. (2002) The grateful disposition: a conceptual and empirical topography. *Journal of Personality and Social Psychology*, 82: 112–27.

McCullough, M.E. and Witvliet, C. v. O. (2000) The psychology of forgiveness. In C.R. Snyder and S.J. Lopez (eds) *Handbook of Positive Psychology.* New York: Oxford University Press.

McDonald, D.G. and Hodgdon, J.A. (1991) *The Psychological Effects of Aerobic Fitness Training: Research and Theory.* New York: Springer-Verlag.

McDougal, J.L., Clonan, S.M. and Martens, B.K. (2000) Using organizational change procedures to promote the acceptability of pre-referral intervention services: the School-Based Intervention Team Project. *School Psychology Quarterly*, 15: 149–71.

McGhee, P. (1999) *Health, Healing and the Amuse System: Humor as Survival Training.* Dubuque, IA: Kendall/Hunt.

McGrath, H. and Noble, T. (2003) *Bounce Back! Teacher's Handbook.* Sydney: Pearson Education.

McQuaid, J. and Carmona, P. (2004) *Peaceful Mind.* Oakland, CA: New Harbinger Publications.

Mishara, B.L. and Ystgaard, M. (2006) Effectiveness of a mental health promotion program to improve coping skills in young children: Zippy's Friends. *Early Childhood Research Quarterly*, 21(1): 110–23.

Moses, J., Steptoe, A., Matthews, A. and Edwards, P. (1989) The effects of exercise training on mental well-being in the normal population: a controlled trial. *Journal of Psychosomatic Research*, 33(1): 47–61.

Nastasi, B.K. (2002) Commentary: the realities of large-scale change efforts. *Journal of Educational and Psychological Consultation*, 13(3): 219–26.

Noble, T. and McGrath, H. (2005) Helping children and families 'bounce back'. *Australian Family Physician*, 9: 34.

Noble, T. and McGrath, H. (in press) Well-being and resilience in education. In S. David and I. Boniwell (eds) *Oxford Handbook of Happiness*. Oxford: Oxford University Press.

Noble, T., McGrath, H., Roffey, S. and Rowling, L. (2008) *A Scoping Study on Student Wellbeing*. Canberra: Australian Government Department of Education, Employment and Workplace Relations.

O'Shaughnessy, T.E., Lane, K.E. Gresham, F.E. and Beebe-Frankenberg, M.E. (2003) Children placed at risk for learning and behavioural difficulties: implementing a school-wide system of early identification and intervention. *Remedial and Special Education*, 24(1): 27–35.

Park, N. and Peterson, C. (2006) Moral competence and character strengths among adolescents: the development and validation of the Values in Action Inventory of Strengths for Youth. *Journal of Adolescence*, 29: 891–909.

Parr, G.D. (1998) Flow theory as a model for enhancing student resilience. *Professional School Counselling*, 1(5): 26–31.

Payton, J., Weissberg, R.P., Durlak, J.A., Dymnicki, A.B., Taylor, R.D., Schellinger, K.B. et al. (2008) *The Positive Impact of Social and Emotional Learning for Kindergarten to Eighth-Grade Students: Findings from Three Scientific Reviews*. Available at: http://www.casel.org/downloads/PackardTR.pdf, Chicago: Collaborative for Academic, Social and Emotional Learning (accessed 11 February 2011).

Pennebaker, J.W. (1997) *Opening Up: The Healing Power of Expressing Emotion*. New York: Guilford Press.

Persaud, R. (2005) *The Motivated Mind*. London: Bantam Books.

Peterson, C. (2006) *A Primer in Positive Psychology*. New York: Oxford University Press.

Peterson, C. and Seligman, M.E.P. (eds) (2003) *Values in Action (VIA) Classification of Strengths and Virtues*. Cincinnati, OH: Values in Action Institute.

Peterson, C. and Seligman, M.E.P. (2004) Humour. In *Character Strengths and Virtues: A Handbook and Classification*. New York: Oxford University Press.

Popovic, N. and Boniwell, I. (2006) Personal Synthesis Programme: bringing psychology to education. In A. Delle Fave (ed.) *Dimensions of Well-Being: Research and Interventions*. Milan: Franco Angeli, pp. 274–93.

Rashid, T. and Anjum, A. (2005) *340 Ways to Use Character Strengths*. Available at: www.viacharacter.org.

Ratey, J.J. (2003) *A User's Guide to the Brain*. London: Abacus.

Ratey, J.J. and Hagerman, E. (2008) *Spark!* London: Quercus.

Reivich, J., Gillham, K., Shatté, A. and Seligman, M.E.P. (2007) *Penn Resiliency Project: A Resilience Initiative and Depression Prevention Programme for Youth and Their Parents*. Executive Summary.

Reivich, K., Seligman, M., Gillham, J., Linkins, M., Peterson, C., Schwartz, B. et al. (2007) *Positive Psychology Programme for High School Students: Lessons for the Pleasant Life, the Good Life and the Meaningful Life*, Positive Psychology for Youth Project, 2007.

Reivich, K. and Shatté, A. (2003) *The Resilience Factor: 7 Keys to Finding Your Inner Strength and Overcoming Life's Hurdles*. New York: Broadway Books.

Reznitskaya, A. and Sternberg, R.J. (2004) Teaching students to make wise judgements: the "Teaching for Wisdom" program. In P.A. Linley and S. Joseph (eds) *Positive Psychology in Practice*. Hoboken, NJ: John Wiley & Sons, pp. 181–96.

Ricard, M. (2006) *Happiness: A Guide to Developing Life's Most Important Skill*. London: Atlantic Books.

Ricciardelli, L.A. (1999) Sociocultural influences on body image, eating and exercise among adolescent boys and girls. *Australian Journal of Psychology: Abstracts of the 34th Annual Conference of the APS*, The Australian Psychological Society, Carlton Sth, Vic.

Roseth, C.J., Johnson, D.W. and Johnson, R.T. (2008) Promoting early adolescents' achievement and peer relationships: the effects of cooperative, competitive and individualistic goal structures. *Psychological Bulletin*, 134(2): 223–46.

Rozin, P. and Royzman, E.B. (2001) Negativity bias, negativity dominance and contagion. *Personality and Social Psychology Review*, 5: 296–320.

Ruch, W. (ed.) (1996) *The Sense of Humour: Explorations of a Personality Characteristic*. New York: Mouton de Gruyter.

Ryan, R.M. and Deci, E.L. (2000) Self-determination theory and the facilitation of instrinsic motivation, social development and well-being. *American Psychologist*, 55: 68–78.

Sacks, O. (2007) *Musicophilia: Tales of Music and the Brain*. London: Picador Books.

Sadeh, A. (2005) Cognitive-behavioral treatment for childhood sleep disorders. *Clinical Psychology Review*, 25: 612–28.

Sadeh, A., Raviv, A. and Gruber, R. (2000) Sleep patterns and sleep disruptions in school age children. *Developmental Psychology*, 36(30): 291–301.

Sallis, J.F., McKenzie, T.L., Kolody, B., Lewis, M., Marshall, S. and Rosengard P. (1999) Effects of health-related physical education on academic achievement: Project SPARK. *Research Quarterly for Exercise and Sport*, 70: 127–134.

Salovey, P., Caruso, D. and Mayer, J.D. (2004) Emotional intelligence in practice. In P.A. Linley and S. Joseph (eds), *Positive Psychology in Practice.* Hoboken, NJ: John Wiley & Sons, pp. 447–463.

Sangsue, J. and Vorpe, G. (2004) Professional and personal influences on school climate in teachers and pupils. *Psychologie du Travail et des Organisations,* 10(4): 341–54.

Sapadin, L. (1997) *It's About Time!: The Six Styles of Procrastination and How to Overcome Them.* London: Penguin.

Saxena, S., Van Ommeren, M., Tang, K.C. and Armstrong, T.P. (2005) Mental health benefits of physical activity. *Journal of Mental Health,* 14: 445–51.

Schaubhut, N.A. (2007) *Technical Brief for the Thomas-Kilmann Conflict Mode Instrument.* Mountain View, CA: CPP, Inc.

Scheckner, S., Rollis, S.A., Kaiser-Ulrey, C. and Wagner, R. (2002) School violence in children and adolescents: a meta-analysis of the effectiveness of current interventions. *Journal of School Violence,* 1(2): 5–32.

Scheier, M.F. and Carver, C.S. (1993) On the power of positive thinking: the benefits of being optimistic. *Current Directions in Psychological Science,* 2: 26–30.

Schmuck, P. and Sheldon, K.M. (2001) *Life Goals and Well-Being: Towards a Positive Psychology of Human Striving.* Kirkland, WA: Hogrefe & Huber Publishers.

Schueller, S.M. (2006) Personality fit and positive interventions: is extraversion important? Unpublished manuscript, Department of Psychology, University of Pennsylvania.

Schwartz, B. (2000) Self-determination: the tyranny of freedom. *American Psychologist,* 55: 79–88.

Segal, Z.V., Williams, J.M.G. and Teasdale, J.D. (2002) *Mindfulness Based Cognitive Therapy for Depression: A New Approach to Preventing Relapse.* New York: Guilford Press.

Seligman, M.E.P. (1991) *Learned Optimism.* New York: Knopf.

Seligman, M.E.P. (2002) *Authentic Happiness.* New York: Free Press.

Seligman, M.E.P. (2007) Coaching and positive psychology. *Australian Psychologist,* 42(4): 266–7.

Seligman, M. and Csikszentmihalyi, M. (2000) Positive psychology: an introduction. *American Psychologist,* 55: 5–14.

Seligman, M.E.P., Ernst, R.M., Gillham, J., Rievich, K. and Linkins, M. (2009) Positive psychology and classroom interventions. *Oxford Review of Education,* 35(3): 293–311.

Seligman, M.E.P. and Peterson, C. (2004) *Character Strengths and Virtues.* New York: Oxford University Press.

Seligman, M.E.P., Rashid, T. and Parks, A.C. (2006) Positive psychotherapy. *American Psychologist,* 61: 774–88.

Seligman, M.E.P., Reivich, K., Jaycox, L. and Gillham, J. (1995) *The Optimistic Child.* New York: Houghton Mifflin.

Seligman, M.E.P., Steen., T., Park, N. and Peterson, P. (2005) Positive psychology progress: Empirical validation of interventions. *American Psychologist,* 60(5): 410–21.

Semple, R.J., Reid, E.F.G. and Miller, L. (2006) Mindfulness-based cognitive therapy for children. In R. Baer (ed.) *Mindfulness-Based Treatment Approaches: Clinician's Guide to Evidence Base and Applications.* New York: Elsevier Academic Press.

Sheldon, K.M. and Lyubomirsky, S. (2006a) How to increase and sustain positive emotion: the effects of expressing gratitude and visualizing best possible selves. *Journal of Positive Psychology,* 1: 73–82.

Shernoff, D.J., Csikszentmihalyi, M., Schneider, B. and Shernoff, E.S. (2003) Student engagement in high school classrooms from the perspective of flow theory. *Psychology Quarterly.* 18: 158–76.

Snyder, C.R., Berg, C., Woodward, J.T., Gum, A., Rand, K.L., Wrobleski, K.K. et al. (2005) Hope against the cold: individual differences in trait hope and acute pain tolerance on the cold pressor task. *Journal of Personality,* 73(2): 287–312.

Snyder, C.R., Rand, K.L., King, E.A., Feldman, D.B. and Woodward. J.T. (2002) 'False' hope. *Journal of Clinical Psychology,* 58(9): 1003–22.

Spillane, M. (2000) *Branding Yourself.* London: Pan Books.

Stallard, P. (2002) *Think Good – Feel Good: A Cognitive Behaviour Therapy Workbook for Children and Young People.* Chichester: John Wiley & Sons.

Steen, T.A., Kachorek, L.V. and Peterson, C. (2003) Character strengths among youth. *Journal of Youth and Adolescence,* 32(1): 5–16.

Steptoe, A., Fieldman, G., Evans, O. and Perry, L. (1996) Cardiovascular risk and responsivity to mental stress: the influence of age, gender and risk factors. *Journal of Cardiovascular Risk,* 3: 83–93.

Steptoe, A., Wardle, J., Pollard, T.M., Canaan, L. and Davies, G.J. (1996) Stress, social support and health-related behavior: a study of smoking, alcohol consumption and physical exercise. *Journal of Psychosomatic Research,* 41(2): 171–80.

Taylor, R. (2003) *The Ultimate Book of Confidence Tricks.* London: Ebury Press.

Thaler, R.H. and Sustein, C.R. (2008) *Nudge: Improving Decisions about Health,* Wealth and Happiness. London: Penguin.

Thomas, K.W. and Kilmann, R.H. (1974) *Thomas-Kilmann Conflict Mode Instrument.* Mountain View, CA: Xicom.

Trost, S.G. (2007) Active education. *Active Living Research Practice,* 10(2): 166–78.

Twenge, J.M. (2007) *Generation Me: Why Today's Young Americans Are More Confident, Assertive, Entitled – And More Miserable Than Ever Before*. New York: Free Press.

UNICEF Innocenti Research Centre (2007) *Child Poverty in Perspective: An Overview of Child Well-Being in Rich Countries*. Available at: www.unicef-irc.org.

Van Gundy, A.B. (1988) *Techniques of Structured Problem-Solving*, 2nd edn. New York: Van Nostrand Reinhold.

Walker, P. (2007) The importance of SEAL: a National Strategies and school perspective, presentation at the Conference of Secondary Head Teachers. Available at: http://www.btandapilot.org.uk/secondary/resources/conference_presentations/peter_walker.ppt.

Warren, J. (2009) *Head Trip*. Methuen: New York.

Weissberg, R.P. and O'Brien, M.U. (2004) What works in school-based social and emotional learning programs for positive youth development. *Annals of the American Academy of Political and Social Science*, 591: 86–97.

Weissberg, R.P., Walberg, H.J., O'Brien, M.U. and Kuster, C.B. (2003) *Long-Term Trends in the Well-Being of Children and Youth*. Washington, DC: CWLA Press.

Wells, J., Barlow, J. and Stewart-Brown, S. (2003) A systematic review of the universal approaches to mental health promotion in schools. *Health Education*, 103(4): 197–220.

Werner, E. and Smith, R. (1992) *Overcoming the Odds: High-Risk Children from Birth to Adulthood*. Ithaca, NY: Cornell University Press.

White, A. (2007) A global projection of subjective well-being: a challenge to positive psychology? *Psychtalk*, 56: 17–20.

Wiseman, R. (2002) *Laughlab: The Scientific Search for the World's Funniest Joke*. London: Random House.

World Health Organization (1947) The constitution of the World Health Organization. *WHO Chronicle*, 1: 6–24.

Yeager, J. (2007) The Culver model – positive psychology and well-being in the independent high school. *Positive Psychology News Daily*, 10 October 2007. Available at: http://pos-psych.com/news/john-yeager/20071010436.

Zapolsky, R.M. (2004) *Why Zebras Don't Get Ulcers*. New York: Owl Books.

Zimbardo, P.G. and Boyd, J.N. (1999) Putting time in perspective: a valid, reliable individual-differences metric, *Journal of Personality and Social Psychology*, 77: 1271–88.

Zins, J.E., Payton, J.W., Weissberg, R.P. and O'Brien, M.U. (2007) Social and emotional learning and successful school performance. In G. Matthews, M. Zeidner and R.D. Roberts (eds) *Emotional Intelligence: Knowns and Unknowns*. New York: Oxford University Press.